INSTANT

FREEZE-DRIED COMPUTER PROGRAMMING IN

★★★★★★★★★★★★★★★★★★★★★★★★★★★★★

B•A•S•I•C

For the Hobbyist, Student, or Compleat Novice. Learn the **NEW** streamlined ALTAIR® style B•A•S•I•C used in personal computers ★ and the similar DEC BASIC-PLUS

BY
JERALD R. BROWN

© Copyright 1977 by DYMAX, Menlo Park, California

Published by dilithium Press, 1978.

10 9 8 7 6 5 4 3

ISBN: 0-918398-21-5

Printed in the United States of America.

dilithium Press
P.O. Box 92
Forest Grove, Oregon 97116

contents

*Designed and produced by the author at DYMAX.
Editing, encouragement, and end of chapter problems
by LeRoy Finkel. Comments and suggestions by
Dragon Emeritus Bob Albrecht. Composer typing
and production management by Mary Jo McPhee.
Cover design and art on pages 3, 4, 8, 48, and 128
by Ann Miya. And thanks to all those who suffered
through the early manuscript to help develop the
instructional sequences and explanations.*

*ALTAIR is the registered trademark of MITS
DEC BASIC PLUS is the registered trademark
    of Digital Equipment Corporation
BASIC is the registered trademark of Dartmouth
    College*

There are dozens of books purporting to teach computer programming in BASIC. Ours is *the greatest* for the following reasons.

- efficiency
- understandability
- economy
- micro/mini oriented, specifically Altair   style BASIC and the similar DEC BASIC PLUS
- no heavy math
- neat little boxed summaries of BASIC throughout the book
- occasional self-tests and activities to see how well we've taught you BASIC

We keep the information coming, but in small, discrete lumps so that you don't choke up.(Hopefully you won't choke with laughter at our humor.)

We take full advantage of the interactive (immediate feedback) quality of BASIC to give you practical demonstrations and practice for fast, easy learning. You get a working familiarity with BASIC in from 6 to 16 hours, fans. Our examples try to keep your typing time to a minimum while maximizing learning and developing good programming techniques.

Our experience teaching beginners from 6 to 60 has shown that there are three programming concepts that sometimes give first-timers problems: conditional branching (IF . . . THEN), looping or iteration (FOR . . . NEXT), and arrays (subscripted variables). We give these concepts special attention using explanations and examples we have refined and found most effective over the years.

We assume that you are a first timer, that you have had no previous programming experience. We assume you have ready access to your own personal computer or a system with BASIC PLUS. Those of you who have had some experience, or have used some of the older versions of BASIC will be able to breeze through the early sections fairly easily.

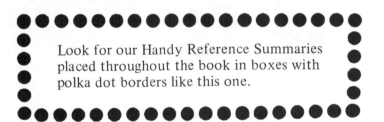

Look for our Handy Reference Summaries placed throughout the book in boxes with polka dot borders like this one.

The first half of the book takes it really slow and easy. We encourage you (in fact, we urge and exhort to the point of browbeating...) to experiment and try out your budding programming skills beyond the examples and projects we include in the book. We want you to think of things interesting to you, and to think of how what you are learning may be applied to such things.

This "active participation" workbook is an alternative to that headache-producing process called "digging it out of the reference manual."

All the programs and RUN's (output) in this book were executed in Altair 8K BASIC version 3.2, which is similar to DEC's BASIC PLUS. Differences in these two versions of BASIC are like dialects of the same BASIC language and are noted in the handy dandy reference boxes.

1

So let's get started. Is the computer turned on? Is the keyboard or Teletype turned on? If not, find someone to show you how to turn them on. In addition, these are the things someone might have to show you in order to get started, if you are new at this game:

(1)   Is the machine (computer) turned on (or "up and running" as they say)?

(2)   If you are using a timesharing system, are you *logged in* to your computer? (Logged in means that a code has been typed into the computer and it is ready to deal with you.)

(3)   Is BASIC ready to use inside your computer? If not, someone must show you how to *call* or *load* and *initialize* BASIC. If you are experienced, and have patience, you might be able to load BASIC into your microcomputer by looking in the reference manual for your system.

The machine or device used to communicate your instructions to the computer, *and* for the computer to communicate with you, will have a typewriter-like keyboard. It's not exactly like a typewriter keyboard, but close. It's called a terminal. Here's some other computer jargon to start chewing on.

The keyboard is an I/O or Input/Output device. It is one of many attachments or *peripherals* that a computer can have. The computer itself, where the computing action takes place, is referred to as a CP or *central processor*. You may also hear CPU or *central processing unit* — same thing.

2

 Ready...

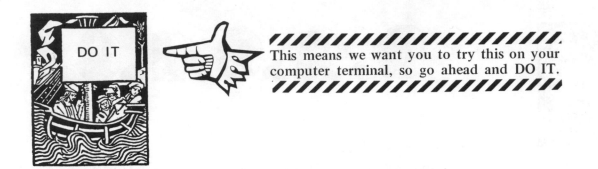

DO IT

This means we want you to try this on your computer terminal, so go ahead and DO IT.

Is your machine up and running in BASIC (turned on and ready)? To get the feel of things, try typing   HELLO COMPUTER

When you have finished typing, press the RETURN or Carriage Return key. Sometimes it is just labelled "CR."

The computer will type out a message in response, such as:

```
HELLO COMPUTER
```
← You type this and hit RETURN.

```
?SN ERROR
OK
```

Computer tells you that you made an error: anything it doesn't understand is considered an error.

SN ERROR means SYNTAX ERROR and it's the computer's way of saying, "Get it right, meathead!"

The point is, the computer didn't understand what you typed. People have not yet designed computers that can figure out from plain English what you want them to do. So to make the computer "do" something, we use a *computer language*, such as BASIC, to present our instructions to the computer.

Set

3

READ

B.A.S.I.C.

This computer language (BASIC) is very simpleminded. BASIC was invented at Dartmouth, and stands for Beginners All-purpose Symbolic Instruction Code. It is designed to make computers easy to program for us non-professionals.

You may have heard of other computer languages, such as FORTRAN, COBOL, APL and many others. Each language gets the computer to do things, but they are designed to make certain uses easier. BASIC is a general purpose language for non-professionals, while COBOL for example, is designed for business-type computer applications, and is used by professional programmers.

BASIC uses English words to communicate instructions to the computer. Although BASIC contains relatively few words and symbols, there is a rather rigid and exact form, or *syntax*, in which these instructions must be presented to the computer. That's what you'll begin learning now.

On most keyboards used for computer terminals, all the letters come out in upper case or capitals *without* using the SHIFT key. Your terminal will either display the *output* on a video screen (CRT) that looks like a television, or else it will print on paper. (CRT stands for Cathode Ray Tube.) Type the word NEW (all in upper case), and then hit the RETURN key. The computer will respond with OK or some similar message.

DO IT

OK

NEW   **You type NEW and hit RETURN.**

OK   **The computer typed this, and then sits there waiting patiently for your next move.**

Any previous instructions that were in the computer's memory have been cleared or erased (or scratched, if you're used to that term) and it is ready to accept NEW instructions.
So type in the following instruction:

```
20 PRINT "THIS IS EASY"
```

and then hit the RETURN key. Here are some Hopefully Helpful Hints:
To get the quotation marks, press the SHIFT key and keep it down while you press ".

If you make a typing error, hit RETURN and start again. You'll learn a better way to make corrections in a few pages.

4

...RUN it

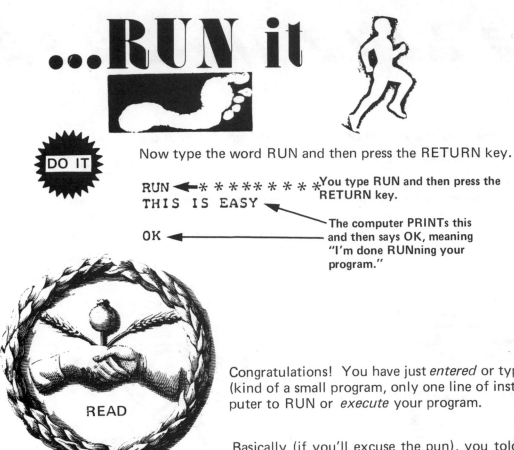

DO IT

Now type the word RUN and then press the RETURN key.

RUN ◄─── * * * * * * * * * You type RUN and then press the RETURN key.

THIS IS EASY ◄─── The computer PRINTs this and then says OK, meaning "I'm done RUNning your program."

OK ◄───

READ

Congratulations! You have just *entered* or typed in a *computer program* (kind of a small program, only one line of instructions), and caused the computer to RUN or *execute* your program.

Basically (if you'll excuse the pun), you told the computer to PRINT what was inside the quotation marks. Your instruction or program was this:

`20 PRINT "THIS IS EASY"`

The computer responded by typing

`THIS IS EASY`

followed by `OK` to tell you it was done.

BY THE LINE NUMBER

READ

Let's get a little more vocabulary out of the way, along with a few of the rules that make up this computer language called BASIC.

When you tell the computer to RUN a program, it starts by following or executing the *statement* or instruction with the smallest *line number.* The instruction you gave to the computer is called a PRINT statement. When you typed RUN and hit RETURN, the computer responded by printing the information between the quotation marks. What is between the quotation marks is called a *string*.

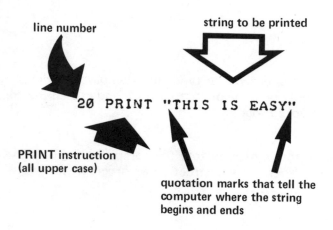

line number

string to be printed

20 PRINT "THIS IS EASY"

PRINT instruction
(all upper case)

quotation marks that tell the
computer where the string
begins and ends

STRING

The little bookworm
crawling up inside
the spine of the
book sez ...

In a BASIC program, an instruction or *indirect statement* such as

20 PRINT "THIS IS EASY"

always begins with a *line number,* which can be any positive number from 1 to 65529. We used 20 as the line number in our example.

A *direct statement* such as NEW and RUN is not part of a program and doesn't being with a line number. Since this book is for teaching you programming instructions, we will talk most about instructions or indirect statements, the kind with the line number. And when we just say "statement", we will be talking about those indirect statements that make up the computers instructions, that is, the program.

When the computer finishes "doing" or executing a statement, it goes on to the next statement in the program in numerical order. That is, the statement with the next larger line number is the next statement *executed.* When you RUN a program, we say the computer *executes* or follows the instructions. That means it does the computing, but not just with numbers.

PRINT

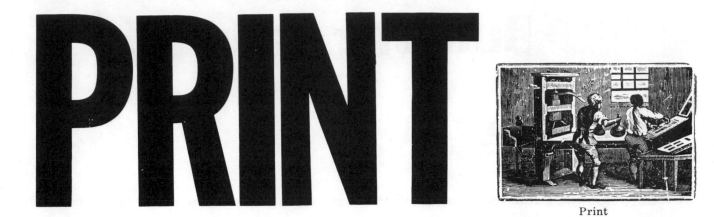

Print

DO IT

First type NEW and hit RETURN. Then type in this program.

```
NEW

OK
10  PRINT "WHAT"
20  PRINT "A"
30  PRINT "BREEZE"
RUN
WHAT
A
BREEZE

OK
```

Hit RETURN at the end of each statement in the program, and also after you type RUN.

First the computer executes Line 10 and PRINTs WHAT.

Then it goes to the statement with the next higher line number, Line 20, and PRINTs A. After Line 20 the computer follows the instruction at the next higher line number, Line 30. Don't tell me, let me guess what it PRINTs.

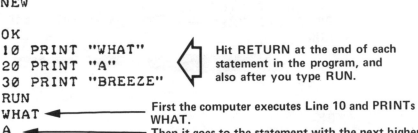

Make your computer talk back to you!

Now you do a program like this one, using the PRINT statement to print one or more strings. Try whole sentences in each string. Don't forget the quotation marks around the string.

```
NEW

OK
```

READ

You don't have to *enter* or type in a program in line number order. That is, you don't have to enter line 10 first, then line 20, and then line 30. If we type in a program *out of line number order,* the computer doesn't care. It follows the line numbers, *not* the order they were *entered* or typed in. This makes it easy to *insert* more statements in a program already stored in the computer's memory. You may have noticed how we cleverly number the statements in our programs by 10's. This makes it easy to add more statements between the existing line numbers -- up to nine more statements between lines 10 and 20, for example.

Computer Tells All!

Now type NEW, hit RETURN, and type in this program. Check the line numbers.

```
NEW

OK
30  PRINT  "BABY"    ◄──── We typed line 30 first, and hit RETURN.
10  PRINT  "TO"     ◄───
20  PRINT  "ME"     ◄───── Then we typed lines 10 and 20.
RUN
TO                          The computer is making advances.
ME        ◄──────────
BABY

OK
```

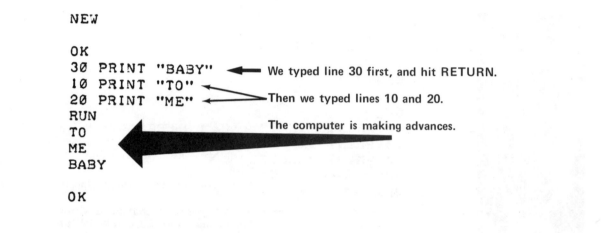

Now type LIST and hit RETURN. See how BASIC has rearranged the program statements into line number order?

```
LIST

10  PRINT  "TO"
20  PRINT  "ME"
30  PRINT  "BABY"
OK
```

LIST tells the computer to LIST the program that you have typed in and stored in its memory. LIST will list each statement in the program in line number order. You can LIST a program any time the computer is not RUNning a program. If you want to see what is in the computer's memory, a penny for your thoughts won't make it, but type LIST and hit RETURN and the computer tells all.

READ

Let's put the PRINT statement through a few tricks so that you get some ideas of what it can do and what it can be used for. First type NEW and hit RETURN. The computer will give you the go ahead sign OK and sit there waiting.

DO IT

NEW — You type NEW and hit RET

OK — BASIC is ready to go to work for you

Use (=/−) for the minus sign.

Use (SHIFT) and (+/;) together for the plus sign.

Then type the following:

```
10 PRINT 12+12
20 PRINT 12-12
```
You carefully type these two lines.

More Hopefully Helpful Hints —

(1) You must hit RETURN when you finish typing an indirect statement and before you type the next line number.

(2) The lower case L does not substitute for the number one (1), and the letter O can't be used for a zero.

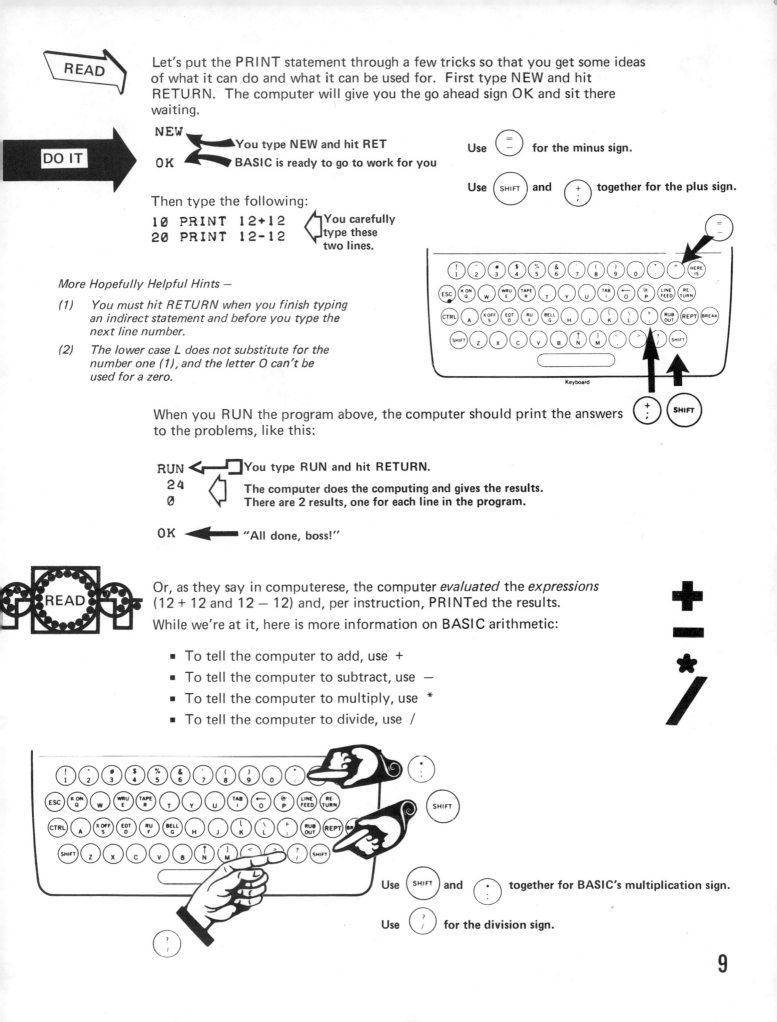

Keyboard

(+/;) (SHIFT)

When you RUN the program above, the computer should print the answers to the problems, like this:

```
RUN
24
0

OK
```

You type RUN and hit RETURN.

The computer does the computing and gives the results. There are 2 results, one for each line in the program.

"All done, boss!"

READ

Or, as they say in computerese, the computer *evaluated* the *expressions* (12 + 12 and 12 − 12) and, per instruction, PRINTed the results.

While we're at it, here is more information on BASIC arithmetic:

- To tell the computer to add, use +
- To tell the computer to subtract, use −
- To tell the computer to multiply, use *
- To tell the computer to divide, use /

Use (SHIFT) and (:/*) together for BASIC's multiplication sign.

Use (?//) for the division sign.

DO IT

First, erase your last program from the computer's memory by typing NEW (and don't forget to press RETURN). Now, type in this program and RUN it.

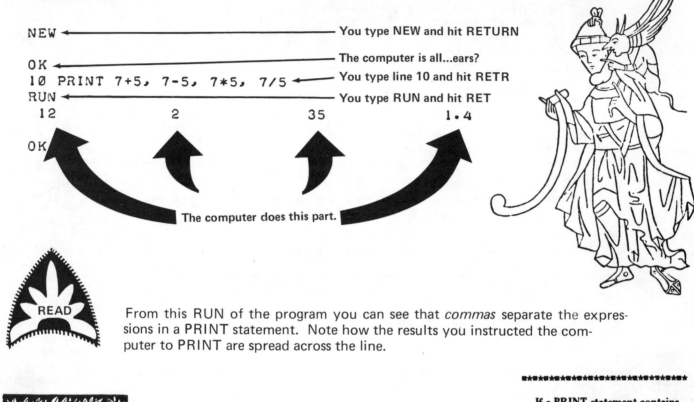

```
NEW  ◄─────────────────────────────── You type NEW and hit RETURN

OK  ◄────────────────────────────────  The computer is all...ears?
10 PRINT 7+5, 7-5, 7*5, 7/5 ◄───────   You type line 10 and hit RETR
RUN  ◄───────────────────────────────  You type RUN and hit RET
   12          2          35          1.4

OK
```

The computer does this part.

READ

From this RUN of the program you can see that *commas* separate the expressions in a PRINT statement. Note how the results you instructed the computer to PRINT are spread across the line.

✱▪✱▪✱▪✱▪✱▪✱▪✱▪✱▪✱▪✱▪✱▪✱

If a PRINT statement contains more than one item. (string or expression), the items must be separated by commas or semicolons.

✱▪✱▪✱▪✱▪✱▪✱▪✱▪✱▪✱▪✱▪✱▪✱

DO IT

Try this one.

✱✱✱✱✱✱✱✱✱✱✱✱✱✱✱

```
NEW

OK
10 PRINT 1*1, 2*2, 3*3, 4*4, 5*5, 6*6, 7*7, 8*8, 9*9
RUN
   1          4          9          16          25
   36         49         64         81

OK
```

PRINT

10

, , , ,

As you can see, using a comma to separate items of expressions in a single PRINT statement gives you five places, columns or *print positions* across the line. There are 72 spaces or *character positions* in a line. (A character is any number, letter, symbol, or single space.) If you are a Doubting Thomas, type X's across a line and keep count.

XXXXXXXXXXXXXXXXXXXXXXXXXXXXXXXXXXXXXXXXXXXXXXXXXXXXXXXXXXXXXXXXXXXXXXXXXX

Some terminals have more than 72 character positions's in a line, and other terminals, especially CRT's (the video screen kind), will have less character positions in a line. Since 72 character lines are most common, we will use that figure in this book.

You say you're a stickler for details? Very well. The comma in the PRINT statement divides the 72 character line into 5 columns, each 14 characters wide. The last two positions on the line are not used.

By the way, BASIC counts the first character space as zero, and the last space as 71, rather than from 1 to 72. (More on that after a while.) For the line below, read the numbers up and down, like this: $\frac{1}{0} = 10 \quad \frac{7}{1} = 71$

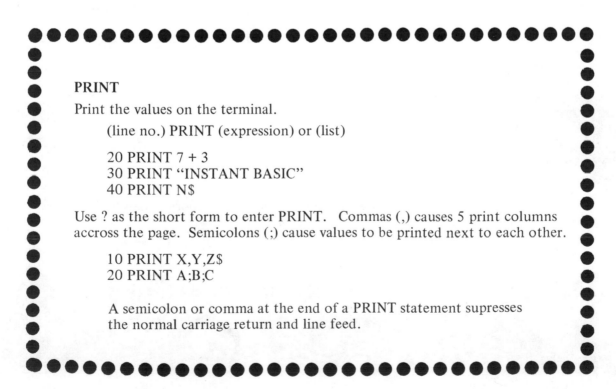

Print Position One

Print Position Two

Print Position Three

Print Position Four

Print Position Five

PRINT

Print the values on the terminal.

(line no.) PRINT (expression) or (list)

20 PRINT 7 + 3
30 PRINT "INSTANT BASIC"
40 PRINT N$

Use ? as the short form to enter PRINT. Commas (,) causes 5 print columns accross the page. Semicolons (;) cause values to be printed next to each other.

10 PRINT X,Y,Z$
20 PRINT A;B;C

A semicolon or comma at the end of a PRINT statement supresses the normal carriage return and line feed.

Now enter (type in) the two statements below. Notice in Line 20 that we are using semicolons instead of commas to separate the expressions.

```
NEW

OK
10  PRINT 7+5,  7-5,  7*5,  7/5
20  PRINT 7+5;  7-5;  7*5;  7/5
RUN
 12              2              35              1.4
 12   2   35   1.4

OK
```

PRINTed by line 10 using commas.

PRINTed by line 20 using semicolons.

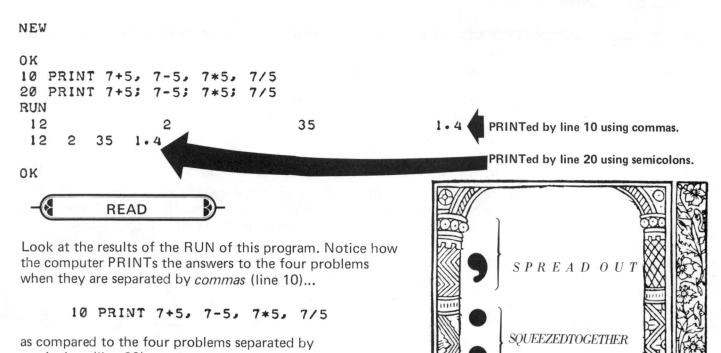

READ

Look at the results of the RUN of this program. Notice how the computer PRINTs the answers to the four problems when they are separated by *commas* (line 10)...

```
10  PRINT 7+5,  7-5,  7*5,  7/5
```

as compared to the four problems separated by *semicolons* (line 20).

```
20  PRINT 7+5;  7-5;  7*5;  7/5
```

, } *SPREAD OUT*

; } *SQUEEZEDTOGETHER*

To tell the computer to squeeze the answers or other output more closely together, use *semicolons* instead of commas. You can use ; and , in the same PRINT statement.

READ

mistrakes

Do you occasionally make mistakes? We do, watch.

```
10 PTINT 2*3+4
RUN
```
We misspell PRINT.

The computer tells use we made a mistake. A check in the reference manual shows us that SN ERROR AT 10 means a syntax mistake; it didn't compute.

```
?SN ERROR IN 10
OK
```

The point is, if we had noticed that we hit T when we meant to hit R, we could have corrected our mistake by using the back arrow or the underline key.

The back arrow ← is on the same key as the letter O. To type a back arrow,

hold the SHIFT key down and press (SHIFT) and (O) together.

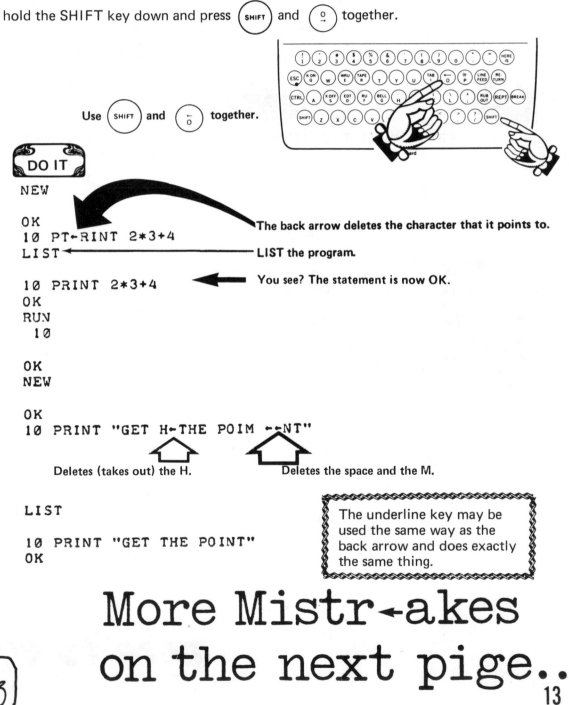

Use (SHIFT) and (←) together.

DO IT

```
NEW

OK
10 PT←RINT 2*3+4
LIST
```
The back arrow deletes the character that it points to.

LIST the program.

```
10 PRINT 2*3+4
OK
RUN
 10

OK
NEW

OK
10 PRINT "GET H←THE POIM ←←NT"
```
You see? The statement is now OK.

Deletes (takes out) the H.   Deletes the space and the M.

```
LIST

10 PRINT "GET THE POINT"
OK
```

The underline key may be used the same way as the back arrow and does exactly the same thing.

More Mistr←akes
on the next pige...

Have you ever considered taking typing lessons?

13

READ

If you have been typing along *entering* a statement and ...suddenly... you want to delete (take out) the *entire line* you were entering, BASIC does allow you to start over. You merely type @ while holding down the SHIFT key.

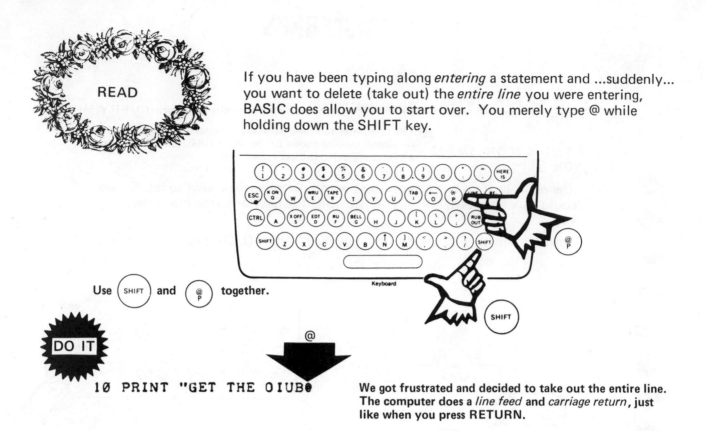

Keyboard

Use (SHIFT) and (@ P) together.

DO IT

@

10 PRINT "GET THE OIUB@

We got frustrated and decided to take out the entire line. The computer does a *line feed* and *carriage return*, just like when you press RETURN.

READ

Let's say that you want to delete (take out) one line of a program that you have already entered into the computer, but you want to save the rest. You *don't* want to use NEW and start over. So what you do is just type the *line number* of the statement you want to remove, and then hit RETURN. First, here is another little program.

```
NEW

OK
10 PRINT "NOT"
20 PRINT "VERY"
30 PRINT "MUCH"
RUN
NOT
VERY
MUCH

OK
```

DO IT

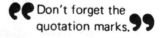 Don't forget the quotation marks. ,,

more to come....

Now we want to take out Line 10 so that the program will only print VERY MUCH. But *don't* type NEW. Follow the instructions below.

```
10
LIST
```
Type the line number and hit RETURN.
Type LIST and RETURN — presto, Line 10 has disappeared forever ... or until you re-enter it.

```
20 PRINT "VERY"
30 PRINT "MUCH"
OK
RUN
VERY
MUCH

OK
```
RUN it.

You may also *replace* a line in a program. To *replace* a statement, type the line number of the statement you wish to replace, and continue with the new statement. When you finish the statement and hit RETURN, your new new line has replaced the old statement.

```
LIST

20 PRINT "VERY"
30 PRINT "MUCH"
OK
```
**We want to replace this line.
(These two statements are still in the computer's memory.)**

```
20 PRINT "TOO"
LIST
```
Type this line with the line number for the statement you want replaced.
LIST to see the modified program.

Our new program is far out . . . .

```
20 PRINT "TOO"
30 PRINT "MUCH"
OK
RUN
TOO
MUCH

OK
```

Too much!

direct mode

READ

Altair-style BASIC has a special *direct mode* that allows you to use a PRINT statement to calculate and PRINT the results for you. You may wish to use direct mode to experiment with BASIC arithmetic. Instead of using a line number, as you do when entering a PRINT statement, you directly type

Look Ma! No line number!

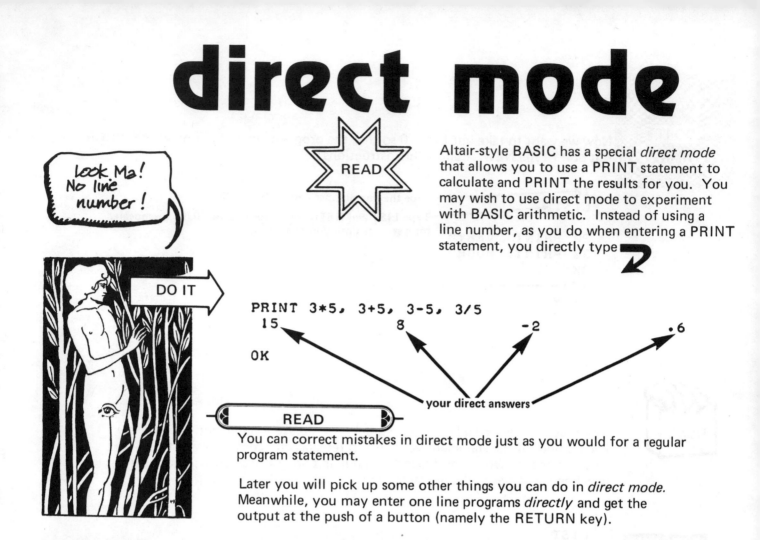

DO IT

```
PRINT 3*5, 3+5, 3-5, 3/5
    15           8              -2              .6

OK
```

your direct answers

READ

You can correct mistakes in direct mode just as you would for a regular program statement.

Later you will pick up some other things you can do in *direct mode*. Meanwhile, you may enter one line programs *directly* and get the output at the push of a button (namely the RETURN key).

Here are some little programs to give you more practice with the PRINT statement and BASIC arithmetic. Try them out. (Bet you thought you were past basic arithmetic ... .)

DO IT

```
NEW

OK
10 PRINT "8 + 2 ="; 8+2      ⟵   This one is tricky!
RUN
8 + 2 = 10

OK
```

```
            10 PRINT "8 + 2 ="; 8+2
```

with " "
This is a string enclosed by quotation marks. The computer does not evaluate the arithmetic instructions inside of a string.

without " "
But the computer does evaluate or compute this because it isn't enclosed by quotes and therefore is not a string.

The semicolon says to print the parts of the PRINT statement close together.

16

How BASIC Figures It.

Enter and RUN the following programs. Or, if you'd rather, use *direct mode* to do each line or each arithmetic problem.

```
NEW

OK
10  PRINT 2*3+4, 2*3+4*5, 2*3/4
20  PRINT 2*(3+4), (2+3)*(4+5), (2+3)/(4+5)
RUN
   10              26              1.5
   14              45              .555556

OK
NEW

OK
10  PRINT 2*2*2*2*2
20  PRINT 2↑5
RUN
   32   2 x 2 x 2 x 2 x 2 is the same as 2⁵
   32   (two to the fifth power). Note the use
        of the up arrow ↑ in BASIC to com-
OK      pute the power of a number.
```

Here's where the up arrow is located.

THE RULES

EXPERIMENT!

1. BASIC *evaluates an expression* (does the arithmetic) by starting at the left side of the expression and working towards the right...

2. ...doing all the power (↑) computations first...†

3. ...then starting at the left again and working right, doing all the multiplications (*) and divisions (/)...

4. ...then starting once again at the left, BASIC works through the expression doing all the additions (+) and subtractions (—).

5. However, BASIC evaluates the expressions *inside* of parentheses ( ) first, following the same Rules of Precedence (who comes first) stated in 1 to 4 above.

6. If there are pairs of parentheses *within* parentheses, the evaluation or computing is done inside the inner-most set of parentheses first, then the computing is done inside the next set of parentheses, and so on and so on.

7. But don't forget: each *left* parenthesis (must have a matching *right* parenthesis), and vice versa, or BASIC will give you an error message when you try to RUN the program.

† Of course you can control the order in which power (↑) or any other calculation is done by using parentheses — see 5, 6 and 7 above. Join the Parentheses Power movement!

HUMAN SOFTWARE

CHAPTER 1 PROBLEMS

ARF

HIS MASTER'S MIND

1. Write a BASIC program that will
   (a) print your name,
   (b) print your street address,
   (c) print your city, state and zip code,

   on three consecutive lines.

2. Rewrite Program 1 in one statement to write all that information on one line across your I/O device (terminal).

3. To erase the program in memory, type _____ and press _____.
   The computer will type _____.

4. To get a print out of your program in memory, type _____

   and press _____.

5. In entering a program, you type PRINY when you meant to type

   PRINT. To correct the mistake, type _____ or _____

   then type T.

6. Use direct mode to balance your checkbook containing these figures:
   Beginning balance: 172.16
   Checks: 13.50, 19.00, 3.25, 10.00, 114.14
   Deposits: 87.57

7. Write a program to compute the average height of the 10 children who came to Danny's birthday party. Their individual heights are (in inches): 40, 50, 46, 48, 49, 45, 52, 41, 44, 45.

   Use this space to write out your programs before you RUN them.

The answers or solutions are in the back of the book (unless your teacher has razored them out...).

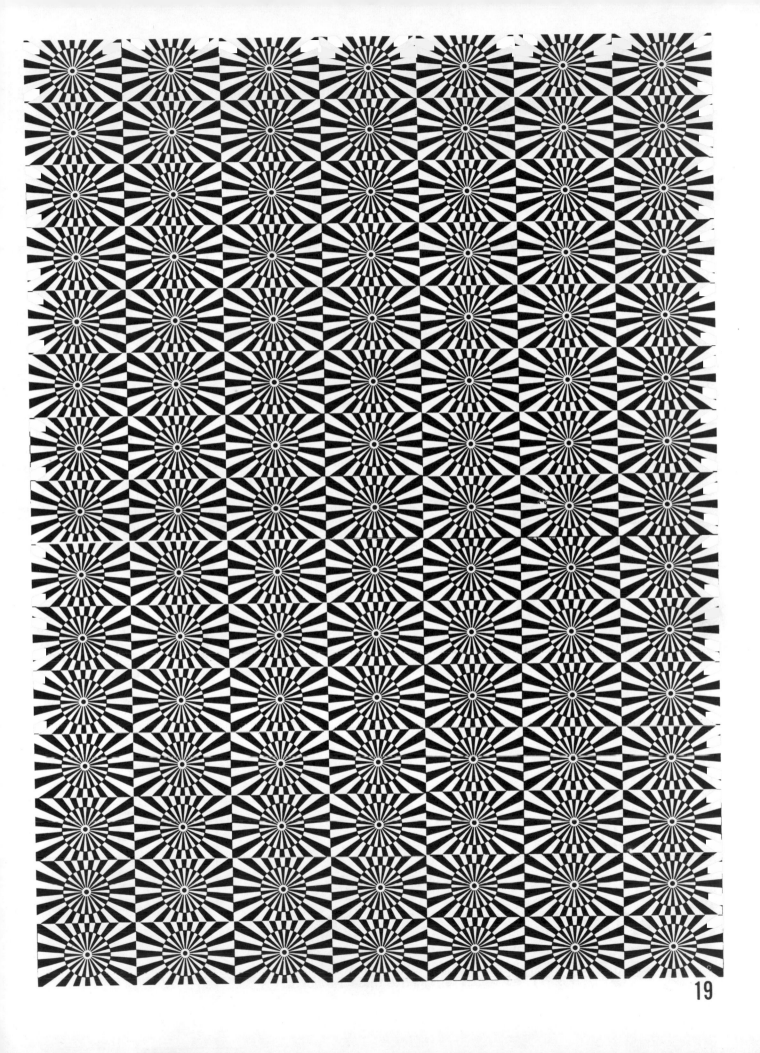

19

READ

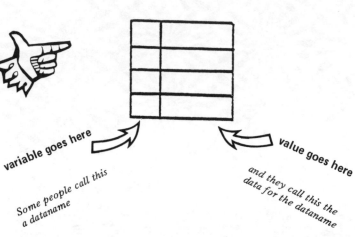

variable goes here

Some people call this a dataname

value goes here

and they call this the data for the dataname

Imagine that down inside the computer there are a bunch of little boxes with two compartments, like this: The left side of each box can hold a label called a *variable*. The right side of each box can hold a number, called the *value* of the variable.

A	32
B	6.5
X	3
P	--10

Here we have some of the boxes with the variable labels filled in, and with values *assigned* to the variables. We have LET variable A have the value 32. That means that the value 32 is *assigned* to the label or variable A, or simply A = 32. Variable B is *assigned* the value 6.5, or B = 6.5. Likewise, X = 3 and P = —10 (minus ten).

DO IT

Here is a way to get the computer to fill in those little boxes, that is, to *assign values to variables*.

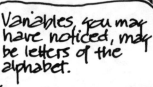 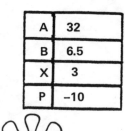

LET

Variables, you may have noticed, may be letters of the alphabet.

```
NEW

OK
10 LET A=32
20 LET B=6.5
30 LET X=3
40 LET P=-10
50 PRINT A, B, X, P
RUN
  32            6.5            3            -10

OK
```

After you RUN the program, the boxes look like this:

A	32
B	6.5
X	3
P	–10

 50 PRINT A, B, X, P This statement does *not* tell the computer to print the letters A, B, X and P, because they are *not* strings enclosed by quotation marks. Instead, this statement tells the computer to PRINT the *values* assigned to these *variables*.

DO IT

Now try this one:

```
NEW

OK
10 LET A=5
20 LET B=10
30 LET A=15
40 PRINT A-B
RUN
 5

OK
```

READ

What?? Two A's being assigned different values by lines 10 and 30? If you look closely, you'll see that the value assigned in Line 30 is the value (15) used in Line 40 to *evaluate* (do the arithmetic) and print the result. BASIC always uses the *last* value assigned to a variable. In effect, any new value assigned to a variable, replaces the former value in the box for the same variable. The old value is lost forever, unless a new assignment is made.

Here is a *trace* of the program as the computer goes through the program in line number order. A trace traces the path the computer uses when RUNning the program, showing the *value* of the variables after each statement is executed by the computer. The computer, in case you haven't noticed, is a fast worker, and starts to print the results of our program almost as soon as you type RUN and hit RETURN.

STATEMENTS	VARIABLES & VALUES	EXPLANATION
10 LET A=5	A 5	The value of A after the computer executes (follows the instruction) in Line 10.
20 LET B=10	A 5 / B 10	The value of A is still 5 after the computer executes Line 20 and assigns the value 10 to variable B.
30 LET A=15	A 15 / B 10	The old value of A is replaced by the new value 15 after the computer executes Line 30. The value of B hasn't changed.
40 PRINT A-B	A 15 / B 10	The values of the variables don't change as the computer executes Line 40. The values in A and B are used by the computer to evaluate A — B and PRINT the result

```
RUN
 5

OK
```

THIS IS A TRACE.

21

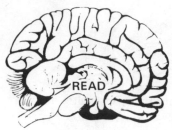

Here's a sharp programmers tip. After you have RUN a program and the computer has finished and answered OK, the values of all variables in the program stay in the boxes. That means you can find out what were the last values for the variables the computer was using when it finished RUNning the program (what values were left in the boxes at the end of the RUN). You find out using *direct mode*. Since direct mode does not use line numbers, it doesn't affect the program you have entered in the computer's memory.

DO IT

Use direct mode to find out what values are still in the computer's memory. (*Don't* type NEW!)

```
PRINT A,B
 15              10

OK
```

Using the trace technique and the direct mode, you may be able to discover *bugs* in your program. But don't get out the bug spray. *Bug* is computer jargon for some mistake in your program. It could be a typing error, an error in using BASIC, or an error in your understanding of how to make the computer do your thing. The motto is, "Keep On Debugging," which will soon be released as a disco single.

As you can see from that last example, a variable can only have one value at a time, and the <u>last</u> value assigned will be the one recorded in the little box for that variable. The previous value is replaced by the latest one assigned, and any previous value of that variable is gone forever.

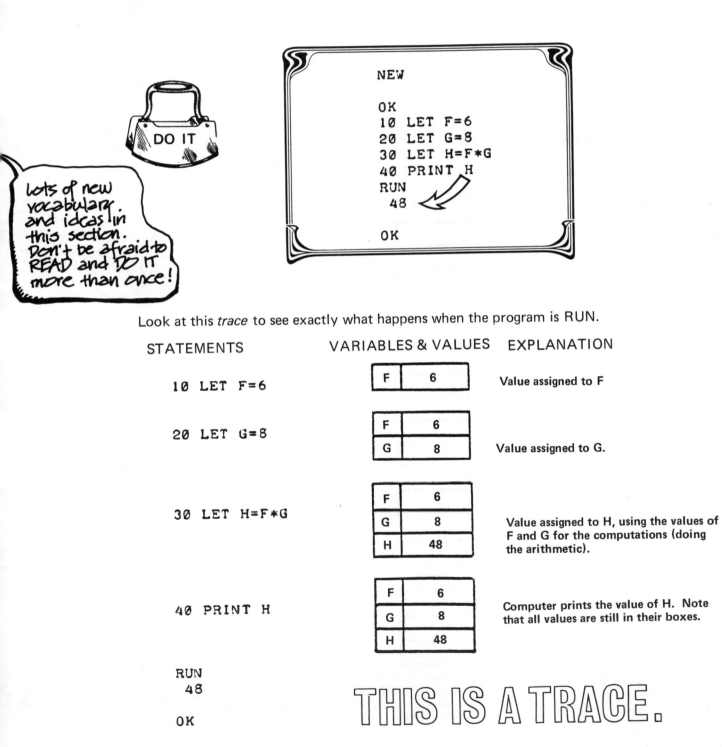

```
NEW

OK
10 LET F=6
20 LET G=8
30 LET H=F*G
40 PRINT H
RUN
   48

OK
```

Lots of new vocabulary and ideas in this section. Don't be afraid to READ and DO IT more than once!

Look at this *trace* to see exactly what happens when the program is RUN.

STATEMENTS	VARIABLES & VALUES	EXPLANATION
10 LET F=6	F 6	Value assigned to F
20 LET G=8	F 6 G 8	Value assigned to G.
30 LET H=F*G	F 6 G 8 H 48	Value assigned to H, using the values of F and G for the computations (doing the arithmetic).
40 PRINT H	F 6 G 8 H 48	Computer prints the value of H. Note that all values are still in their boxes.

```
RUN
   48

OK
```

THIS IS A TRACE.

23

More practice? O.K.

```
NEW

OK
10 LET A=2
20 LET B=3
30 LET C=4
40 LET D=5
50 PRINT A+B+C+D, A*B*C*D, A*(B+C), (A+B)/(C+D)
RUN
 14             120            14            .555556

OK
```

$$\frac{A+B}{C+D}$$

L E T

Now, you do a trace for this program.

STATEMENTS	VARIABLES & VALUES	EXPLANATION
10 LET A=2	A ⬚	
20 LET B=3	A ⬚ B ⬚	
30 LET C=4	A ⬚ B ⬚ C ⬚	
40 LET D=5	A ⬚ B ⬚ C ⬚ D ⬚	
50 PRINT A+B+C+D, ETC.	A ⬚ B ⬚ C ⬚ D ⬚	

Did you remember? The values of variables don't change when a PRINT statement is executed, even if the values are used in computations (doing arithemetic problems).

Don't forget to experiment! Do it today!

24

Eight Bend.   Jam Hitch.   Double Hitch.   Loop on Knot.

READ

However, there is more to variables than just putting numbers in boxes. Instead of a number, the value of a variable can be a *string*. So that BASIC knows that we are dealing with a *string variable*, the label or variable name ends with a $, for example, A$ in a LET statement. The string that is being assigned to the string variable is enclosed by quotation marks, just as in a PRINT statement.

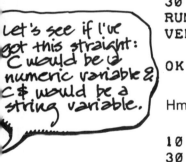

DO IT

Strings?

```
NEW

OK
10 LET C$="VERY"
20 LET E$="GOOD"
30 PRINT C$; C$; E$
RUN
VERYVERYGOOD

OK
```

C$	VERY
E$	GOOD

Well, we could try it another way. Without typing NEW, *replace* Line 30 with a new Line 30, using commas where the semicolons were.

Let's see if I've got this straight: C would be a numeric variable & C$ would be a string variable.

```
30 PRINT C$, C$, E$
RUN
VERY            VERY            GOOD

OK
```

Hmmmm, still not too good. Replace Lines 10 and 30 like this

```
10 LET C$="VERY "        see the extra space
30 PRINT C$; C$; E$
LIST                semicolons again

10 LET C$="VERY "
20 LET E$="GOOD"
30 PRINT C$; C$; E$
OK
RUN
VERY VERY GOOD

OK
```

READ

We hope this last exercise has given you some ideas about how to assign strings to string variables, and some of the techniques you may use when you want to put strings together in a PRINT statement. Of course there is more to be said about strings, and you can bet that we will say a lot of it!

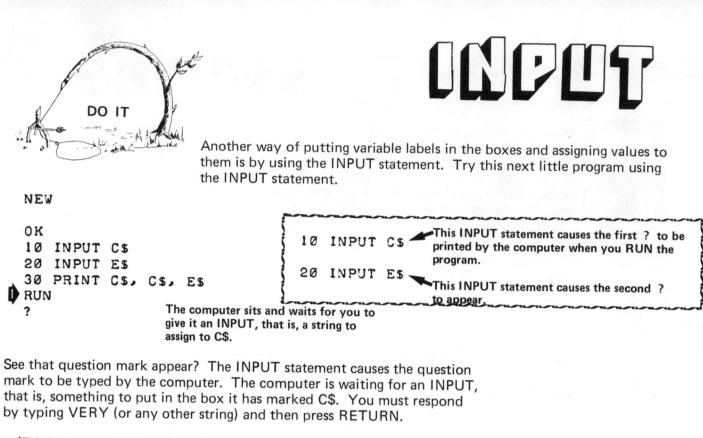

DO IT

Another way of putting variable labels in the boxes and assigning values to them is by using the INPUT statement. Try this next little program using the INPUT statement.

```
NEW

OK
10 INPUT C$
20 INPUT E$
30 PRINT C$, C$, E$
RUN
?
```

```
10 INPUT C$    ← This INPUT statement causes the first ? to be printed by the computer when you RUN the program.

20 INPUT E$    ← This INPUT statement causes the second ? to appear.
```

The computer sits and waits for you to give it an INPUT, that is, a string to assign to C$.

See that question mark appear? The INPUT statement causes the question mark to be typed by the computer. The computer is waiting for an INPUT, that is, something to put in the box it has marked C$. You must respond by typing VERY (or any other string) and then press RETURN.

(This is the same RUN continued.)

```
RUN
? VERY
?
```

We typed VERY and hit RETURN.

C$	VERY

The computer has made C$ = VERY. Then the INPUT statement in Line 20 causes the second ? to be printed, and again the computer waits for an INPUT to assign to E$.

Another question mark? Yes, now Line 20 of the program tells the computer to ask for a string for E$, and it awaits your fancy. Type GOOD (or be original) and hit RETURN.

(Still the same RUN, folks.)

```
RUN
? VERY
? GOOD
VERY      VERY      GOOD

OK
```

We typed GOOD and hit RETURN.

E$	GOOD

The computer executes Line 30 and PRINTs this.

And old reliable prints the string labeled C$ twice, and the string corresponding to E$ once, just as the PRINT statement (Line 30) tells it to.

If we want spaces before or after the string we are entering after an INPUT question mark, we just enter the string with quotation marks around it. We could enter the word VERY enclosed by quotation marks and include a space in the string. First, change line 30 so that the string variables are separated by semicolons instead of commas, then RUN the program again.

```
30 PRINT C$; C$; E$
RUN
? "VERY "
? GOOD
VERY VERY GOOD

OK
```

Hi! I'm an INPUT question mark waiting for you!

26

READ

But that question mark isn't too informative by itself. You don't know what to respond to an INPUT question mark unless you know what the program is about. So here is how you provide a prompt or cue as to what the program needs for an INPUT.

DO IT

```
NEW

OK
10 INPUT "WHAT IS YOUR NAME"; N$
20 PRINT N$; " IS YOUR NAME."
```

Note the semicolon

Note the space

Note the semicolon

Tell the computer your name (type it in, silly, and don't forget RETURN) when it asks you.

It asks   You respond

```
RUN
WHAT IS YOUR NAME? JERALD R. BROWN
JERALD R. BROWN IS YOUR NAME.

OK
```

N$	JERALD R. BROWN

Your INPUT string is assigned to N$.

READ

Note that you must put the INPUT string

"WHAT IS YOUR NAME"

in quotation marks, and that between the INPUT *string* and the INPUT *variable* you *must* use a semicolon (;).

```
10 INPUT "WHAT IS YOUR NAME"; N$
```

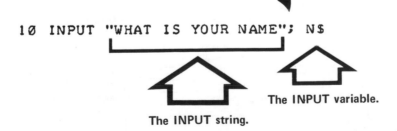

The INPUT string.

The INPUT variable.

more to come....

READ

We tried it with a comma, and here's what happened: (Don't do it, just look at what we did for a change)

```
10 INPUT "WHAT IS YOUR NAME", N$
RUN

?SN ERROR IN 10
OK
```

Well, BASIC didn't like that at all. It's that nasty Syntax Error message.

Also, if you'll check Line 20 of our program, you'll notice we use a semicolon in the PRINT statement so that all the parts of the PRINT statement would be squeezed close together.

```
20 PRINT N$; " IS YOUR NAME."
```

(Want to try it with a comma to see the difference?)

I am not a string, so don't thread on me!

Now, without typing NEW, add lines 30 and 40 to the program. Then RUN it and have a short conversation with your computer!

We used a numeric variable since the program is asking for a number. But it would have been all right to use a string variable since the number will not be used in any calculations.

```
30 INPUT "HOW OLD ARE YOU"; A
40 PRINT N$; ", YOU ARE"; A; "YEARS OLD."
```

Note the comma and space inside of the quotation marks.

```
RUN
WHAT IS YOUR NAME? JACK
JACK IS YOUR NAME.
HOW OLD ARE YOU? 24
JACK, YOU ARE 24 YEARS OLD.
```

Someone typed their name and age after the question marks.

```
OK
```

Now LIST the program if you want to see it all together.

```
LIST

10 INPUT "WHAT IS YOUR NAME"; N$
20 PRINT N$; " IS YOUR NAME."
30 INPUT "HOW OLD ARE YOU"; A
40 PRINT N$; ", YOU ARE"; A; "YEARS OLD."
OK
```

who's old-fashioned?

Another way to enter a program that does pretty much the same thing. This is the old fashioned way. Isn't Altair-style BASIC nice?

```
NEW

OK
10 PRINT "WHAT IS YOUR NAME";  ◄─ Note these semicolons, which tell the
20 INPUT N$                        computer to stay on the same line
30 PRINT N$; " IS YOUR NAME."      when it has finished PRINTing what
40 PRINT "HOW OLD ARE YOU";        it was told to.  Then the INPUT
50 INPUT A                         statement supplies the question mark.
60 PRINT N$; ", YOU ARE"; A; "YEARS OLD."
RUN
WHAT IS YOUR NAME? BILL
BILL IS YOUR NAME.
HOW OLD ARE YOU? 22
BILL, YOU ARE 22 YEARS OLD.

OK
```

N$	BILL
A	22

LET
Assigns a value to a numeric variable or a string variable. LET is optional.

(line no.) LET (variable) = (expression)

```
10 LET X = 3
20 LET Z = X*5
30 N$ = "NAME"
```

BASIC PLUS only
```
10 LET X,Y,Z = 33  —  multiple LET, all values = 33
```

INPUT
Requests data from the terminal (?)

INPUT (varaible name(s)) or (list)
INPUT ("string") ; (variable name(s))

```
10 INPUT X
20 INPUT X,Y,Z
30 INPUT "WHAT IS YOUR NAME" ; N$
```

READ

READ and DATA~They

You can get the computer to fill in those little boxes, that is, *assign value to variables,* in yet a third way. First, we used LET. Then we used INPUT. Now we use READ and DATA. This method uses the combination of two BASIC statements that *always* work together. They're real pals, the READ statement and DATA statement. Actually, they can be more like a gang, with READ as the leader, and lots of DATA followers.

Try any version of the program below to see how the two statements work together to assign values *or* strings to variables. To make it simple at first, we just use one data item, either a *value* or a *string,* in the DATA statement.

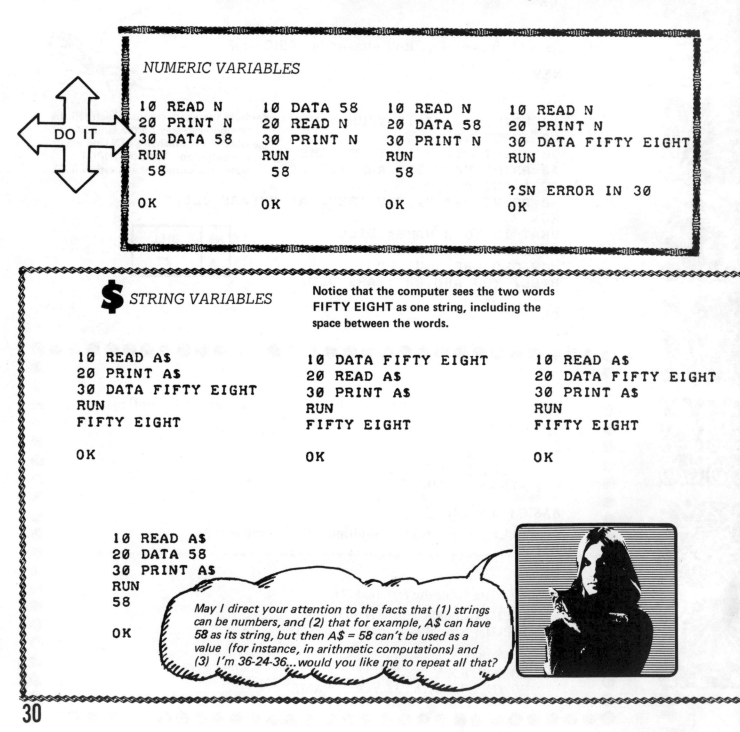

NUMERIC VARIABLES

DO IT

```
10 READ N        10 DATA 58       10 READ N        10 READ N
20 PRINT N       20 READ N        20 DATA 58       20 PRINT N
30 DATA 58       30 PRINT N       30 PRINT N       30 DATA FIFTY EIGHT
RUN              RUN              RUN              RUN
  58               58               58

                                                  ?SN ERROR IN 30
OK               OK               OK               OK
```

$ *STRING VARIABLES*

Notice that the computer sees the two words **FIFTY EIGHT** as one string, including the space between the words.

```
10 READ A$       10 DATA FIFTY EIGHT       10 READ A$
20 PRINT A$      20 READ A$                20 DATA FIFTY EIGHT
30 DATA FIFTY EIGHT  30 PRINT A$           30 PRINT A$
RUN              RUN                       RUN
FIFTY EIGHT      FIFTY EIGHT               FIFTY EIGHT

OK               OK                        OK
```

```
10 READ A$
20 DATA 58
30 PRINT A$
RUN
58

OK
```

May I direct your attention to the facts that (1) strings can be numbers, and (2) that for example, A$ can have 58 as its string, but then A$ = 58 can't be used as a value (for instance, in arithmetic computations) and (3) I'm 36-24-36...would you like me to repeat all that?

work together to assign values and strings to variables.

READ

As you can see from these examples, the READ statement will assign the value or string in the DATA statement to its variable (the READ variable). No matter where the DATA statement is placed in the program (first, last, or in the middle), the computer assigns the first item in the first DATA statement to the first READ variable.

DO IT

```
NEW

OK
10 READ A$, B$, C$
20 PRINT C$, B$, A$
30 DATA GREAT, THIS, AIN'T
RUN
AIN'T          THIS          GREAT

OK
```

READ

Looking at the last example, notice that the items in a DATA statement are separated by *commas*, but there is *no comma* after the last item.

Note commas   **Note lack of comma**

```
30 DATA GREAT, THIS, AIN'T
```

Note that spaces are not counted as part of the string unless the space is between words in the same string item. *Leading* **spaces are ignored.** *Trailing* **spaces ignored. But** *imbedded* **spaces are part of the string.**

31

10 READ X$, Y$, Z$, K, L

Now try the next program, which shows that a single READ statement can be used to assign both numerical values and strings to the appropriate READ variables in the same READ statement.

```
NEW

OK
10 READ B$, C$, A, B, C
20 PRINT A; B$; B; B$; C; C$; A+B+C
90 DATA ADDED TO, GIVES YOU, 5, 8, 10
RUN
 5 ADDED TO 8 ADDED TO 10 GIVES YOU 23

OK
```

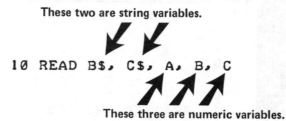

These two are string variables.

These three are numeric variables.

The computer assigns the strings and/or the numerical values in the DATA statement, one at a time, to the variables in the READ statement. However, the computer is quite particular. It will only assign numerical values to numerical variables (those *without* the $). String variables (those *with* the $ at the end) will accept numbers as strings, as well as words and some symbols such as punctuation marks. But the computer won't pick and choose. The DATA must be in the same order as the variables: numerical values for numerical variables and strings for string variables. Got that? Notice again that each item in the DATA statement is separated by a comma, but there is no comma after the last item.

Replace Line 10 in the last program with this Line 10. Why won't it RUN?

```
10 READ A, B, C, B$, C$
```

(If you wish to check for the entire program, type LIST. If you have faith, just type RUN.)

```
LIST

10 READ A, B, C, B$, C$
20 PRINT A; B$; B; B$; C; C$; A+B+C
90 DATA ADDED TO, GIVES YOU, 5, 8, 10
OK
RUN

?SN ERROR IN 90
OK
```

Notice that the computer thinks that you made an error in the order that you entered the data in the DATA statement.

Like we said, the READ statement won't pick and choose among the items in a DATA statement. The items in the DATA must be in the same order as the variables — numbers only for regular variables and strings for string variables (the ones with the $ after the letter of the alphabet).

Another thing you should know about DATA statements: Even if several READ statements are used in a program they take their values in turn from the same DATA statement. When all the DATA in one DATA statement is used up, that is, when all the items have been assigned just once to variables, the computer goes on to the next DATA statement. Even if they are located in different places in a program, the computer looks for DATA statements in line number order, and takes the DATA statement with the smallest line number as the first one.

How's your typing?

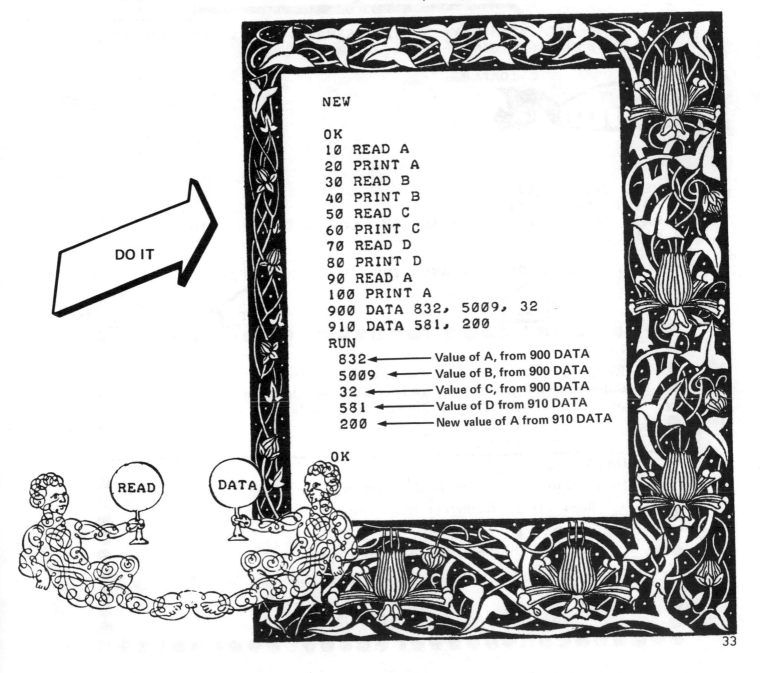

DO IT

```
NEW

OK
10  READ A
20  PRINT A
30  READ B
40  PRINT B
50  READ C
60  PRINT C
70  READ D
80  PRINT D
90  READ A
100 PRINT A
900 DATA 832, 5009, 32
910 DATA 581, 200
RUN
  832 ◄———— Value of A, from 900 DATA
  5009 ◄———— Value of B, from 900 DATA
  32 ◄———— Value of C, from 900 DATA
  581 ◄———— Value of D from 910 DATA
  200 ◄———— New value of A from 910 DATA

OK
```

READ   DATA

On Using Quotation Marks in DACA Statements

READ

READ and DATA statements work the same way for strings. One little thing to notice — if you want to have a string with commas in it, you must use quotation marks, just as you do in LET statements or INPUT strings.

first item
second item

```
30 DATA "PARSLEY, SAGE, ROSEMARY, AND WINE", ARE FINE
40 DATA TO DINE
```

third DATA item

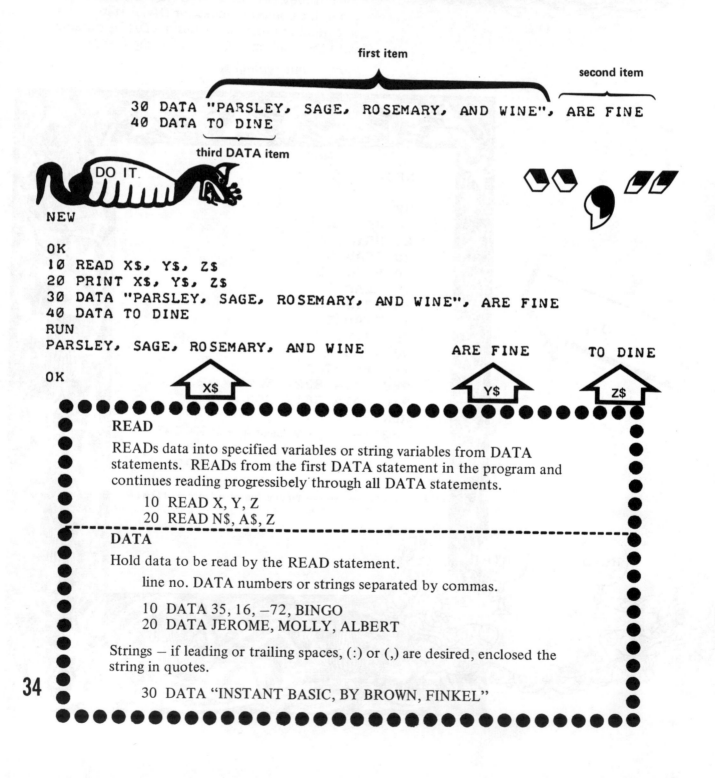

```
NEW

OK
10 READ X$, Y$, Z$
20 PRINT X$, Y$, Z$
30 DATA "PARSLEY, SAGE, ROSEMARY, AND WINE", ARE FINE
40 DATA TO DINE
RUN
PARSLEY, SAGE, ROSEMARY, AND WINE     ARE FINE     TO DINE

OK
```

X$ Y$ Z$

READ

READs data into specified variables or string variables from DATA statements. READs from the first DATA statement in the program and continues reading progressibely through all DATA statements.

```
10  READ X, Y, Z
20  READ N$, A$, Z
```

DATA

Hold data to be read by the READ statement.

line no. DATA numbers or strings separated by commas.

```
10  DATA 35, 16, −72, BINGO
20  DATA JEROME, MOLLY, ALBERT
```

Strings — if leading or trailing spaces, (:) or (,) are desired, enclosed the string in quotes.

```
30  DATA "INSTANT BASIC, BY BROWN, FINKEL"
```

SPACED OUT STRINGS

READ

Another time you must use quotation marks in DATA statements is when you want one or more spaces *before* or after the characters in the string. As we saw earlier, spaces between words or characters are included in the string.

It's just if you want spaces *before* or *after* the string that you must use quotation marks in a DATA statement. Check it out.

DO IT

Type in this program, then RUN it and its several modifications.

```
NEW

OK
10 READ A$, B$, C$
20 PRINT C$; B$; A$
30 DATA GREAT,THIS,AIN'T      ←——— three strings in a DATA statement tra la . . .
RUN
AIN'TTHISGREAT        ←— not so great really . . .

OK
```

```
30 DATA GREAT, THIS, AIN'T     ←— replace Line 30 with a DATA statement that has spaces before
RUN                                or after the string items.
AIN'TTHISGREAT       ←——————
                                   the spaces were not included in the strings assigned
                                   to the string variables. But do not despair...
OK
```

```
30 DATA GREAT, " THIS ", AIN'T        replace Line 30 again with an item of DATA that uses quotation
RUN                                   marks around the string item to tell the computer to include
AIN'T THIS GREAT                      spaces before and after the word as part of the string.

OK                    It worked!
LIST
```

```
10 READ A$, B$, C$
20 PRINT C$; B$; A$
30 DATA GREAT, " THIS ", AIN'T
OK
```

The computer is informed that we want everything inside the quotation marks included in this string, and that means spaces too.

1. Name the three statement types that are used to assign values to a variable (numeric or string). _____ , _____ , _____ .

2. When you use a LET statement, string variable information must be enclosed _____ .

3. After a program is run, the variables still contain the last value. How do you find out these values? _____ .

4. Fill in the trace boxes.

                                  A   B   C   D

```
10 LET A = 12
20 LET B = 14
30 READ C
40 PRINT A + C
50 LET D = B + C/6
60 PRINT D
70 DATA 16, 13, 14
```

5. Write a program to read and print the information in this DATA statement.

DATA SHERRY DELIGHT, 800-555-1212, 23

6. Write a program that 'prompts' the user to enter name, birthdate and astrological sign. Then print the output shown below.

SHERRY DELIGHT, YOUR SIGN IS LEO SINCE YOU WERE BORN 8/15/60.

7. A new water saving device for your toilet claims to save 150 gallons of water per month per toilet. Its cost is $4.80. Water costs about $0.48 per 100 cubic feet.

(a) How long in months, will it take to 'pay off' the purchase price of this device in water used (or not used)?

(b) The device has only a 12 month guarantee against falling apart. Is the purchase worth while in purely economic terms?

(You can and should apply this same problem solving logic to other energy saving devices on the market.)

8. In this era of energy shortage and water drought, we on the West coast are becoming extremely conscious of energy consumption and would like to share our ideas with you (your turn is coming!). In terms of water, we know the facts and figures and many families measure water in terms of flushes per day and things like that. Below is a table of average consumption of various activities. Your exact figures will likely be a bit different and we encourage you to change the table to suit you. Use the table and your handy computer to write a program to compute the average amount of water used by your family per month. Use INPUT statements to enter the variables and DATA statements to contain the constants (from the table). This may be a long program, but it really isn't that difficult.

shower	6 gallons/minute	tub bath	20 gallons
dishwashing	15 gallons	dishwasher	16 gallons
toilet flush	6 gallons		(check yours)
outdoor watering	average hose	washing	
	10 gal./minute	machine	35 gallons
various	you guess/day		

Once the program works, you can change data (reduce flushes, showers, etc.) and see how much water you can save. (Some Marin County, California families are restricted to 40-45 gallons per person per day. Can you swing that?)

loopdeloop

Loop to Line.

Double Loop.

Or in other words, GOTO...

DO IT

Enter this little gem in your trusty computer: (or was that your testy computer . . .)

```
NEW

OK
10 PRINT "THIS IS A LOOP."
20 GOTO 10
```

GOTO 10 tells the computer to "go to" the statement with line number 10, and to continue RUNning the program from there in normal line number order.

Wait! Stop! Halt! Cease! Desist!

Before you RUN it, look for the CONTROL (CTRL) key, and the key of C.

Found them? OK, now RUN the program. When you get tired of watching the output, depress the CONTROL key and the C key *at the same time,* to stop the computer from RUNning the program.

```
RUN
THIS IS A LOOP.
THIS IS A LOOP.
THIS IS A LOOP.
THIS IS A LOOP.
THIS IS A LOOP.
THIS IS A LOOP.
THIS IS A LOOP.
THIS IS A LOOP.

BREAK IN 10
OK
```

Press (CTRL) and (C) together!

We pressed CTRL and C together.

The computer tells you at what line number CONTROL/C broke into the program. If it had kept RUNning, it would have executed Line 10 next.

Common Dropper Loop.

Don't panick! Press CTRL/C.

Loop Bend.

READ

The computer executed Line 10 over and over again, because the GO TO statement in Line 20 told the computer to go back to Line 10 every time it finished executing Line 10 and got to Line 20 again. This is an *infinite loop* — it just goes on running in circles, repeating itself, forever, or until some clever person presses CONTROL and C at the same time.

Use CONTROL/C any time you wish to interrupt or stop the computer from RUNning a program.

37

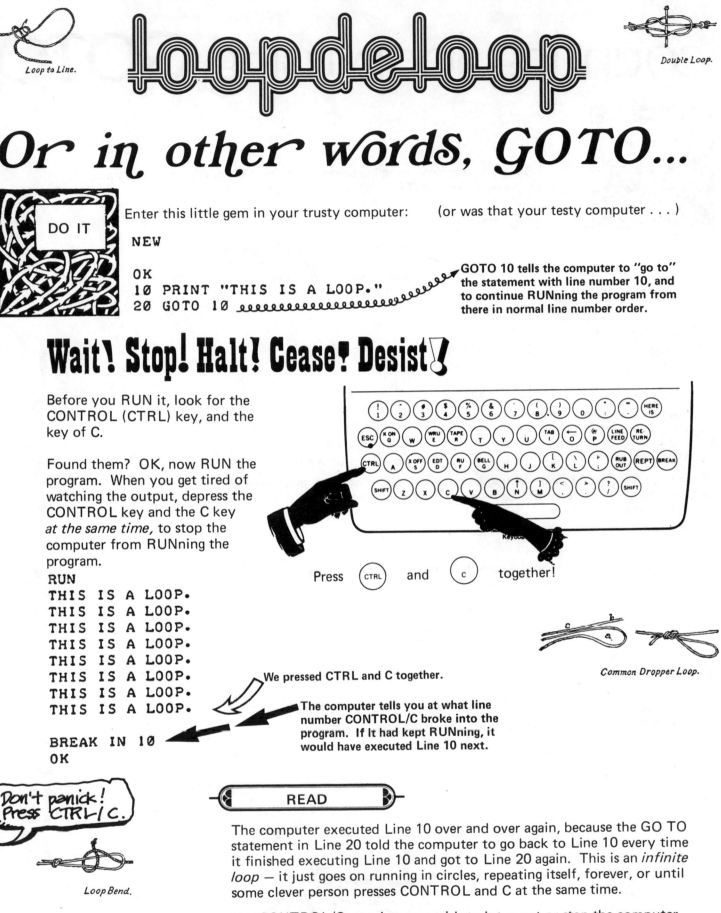

counting loop using GOTO

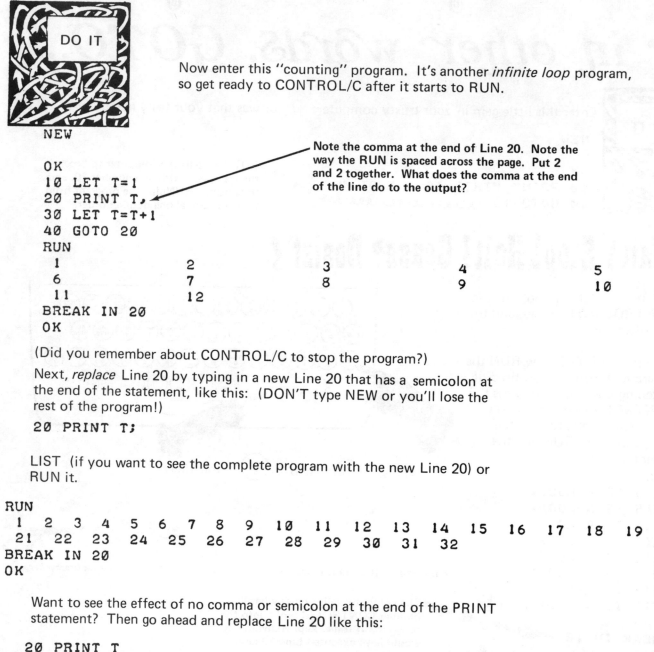

DO IT

Now enter this "counting" program. It's another *infinite loop* program, so get ready to CONTROL/C after it starts to RUN.

```
NEW

OK
10  LET T=1
20  PRINT T,
30  LET T=T+1
40  GOTO 20
RUN
 1              2              3              4              5
 6              7              8              9              10
 11            12
BREAK IN 20
OK
```

Note the comma at the end of Line 20. Note the way the RUN is spaced across the page. Put 2 and 2 together. What does the comma at the end of the line do to the output?

(Did you remember about CONTROL/C to stop the program?)

Next, *replace* Line 20 by typing in a new Line 20 that has a semicolon at the end of the statement, like this: (DON'T type NEW or you'll lose the rest of the program!)

```
20 PRINT T;
```

LIST (if you want to see the complete program with the new Line 20) or RUN it.

```
RUN
 1  2  3  4  5  6  7  8  9  10  11  12  13  14  15  16  17  18  19  20
 21  22  23  24  25  26  27  28  29  30  31  32
BREAK IN 20
OK
```

Want to see the effect of no comma or semicolon at the end of the PRINT statement? Then go ahead and replace Line 20 like this:

```
20 PRINT T
RUN
 1
 2
 3
 4
 5
 6
 7
 8

BREAK IN 20
OK
```

38

1
2
3
4
5
6
7
8
9
10
11

Let's follow along as the computer RUNs that last program. Follow the arrows through the program.

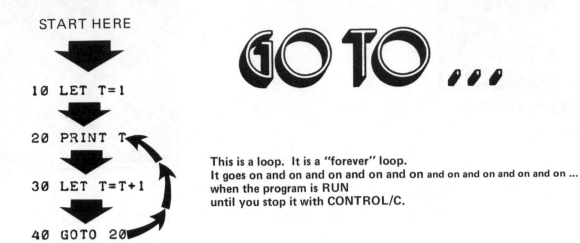

START HERE

```
10 LET T=1

20 PRINT T

30 LET T=T+1

40 GOTO 20
```

This is a loop. It is a "forever" loop.
It goes on and on and on and on and on and on and on and on and on ...
when the program is RUN
until you stop it with CONTROL/C.

Here's another way to look at it, a *trace* of the program. Remember, a *trace* traces the path the computer takes through the program it is working on, and shows you what values are assigned to the variables at any step in the program. In the column marked T we show the value of T after the statement on the same line has been carried out by the computer. In other words, we show what value is in the box labelled T after each statement has been executed. You can think of it as always being the same little box for the same variable T — only the value assigned to T changes from time to time.

STATEMENT	VARIABLES & VALUES	EXPLANATION
10 LET T=1	T 1	Assign T the value 1
20 PRINT T	T 1	Print the value of T.
30 LET T=T+1	T 2	Increase T by 1 (add 1 to the old value of T).
40 GOTO 20	T 2	Go to beginning of loop.
20 PRINT T	T 2	Print the value of T.
30 LET T=T+1	T 3	Increase T by 1.
40 GOTO 20	T 3	Go to beginning of loop.
20 PRINT T	T 3	Print the value of T.
30 LET T=T+1	T 4	Increase T by 1.
40 GOTO 20	T 4	Go to beginning of loop.

etcetera, etcetera, etcetera

THIS IS A TRACE

39

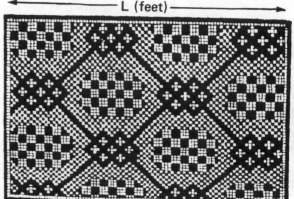

L (feet)

W (feet)

```
NEW

OK
10 INPUT "LENGTH OF FLOOR IN FEET"; L
20 INPUT "WIDTH IN FEET"; W
30 PRINT "YOU NEED"; (L*W)/9; "SQ. YARDS OF CARPET."
40 PRINT
50 GOTO 10
RUN
LENGTH OF FLOOR IN FEET? 12
WIDTH IN FEET? 10
YOU NEED 13.3333 SQ. YARDS OF CARPET.

LENGTH OF FLOOR IN FEET? 16
WIDTH IN FEET? 18
YOU NEED 32 SQ. YARDS OF CARPET.

LENGTH OF FLOOR IN FEET? 16
WIDTH IN FEET? 24
YOU NEED 42.6667 SQ. YARDS OF CARPET.

LENGTH OF FLOOR IN FEET?

OK
```

Blank line courtesy of Line 40.

Hit RETURN to get out of a RUN that has stopped at an INPUT statement. BASIC PLUS Users: Use CONTROL/C. Hitting RETURN assigns a zero to numeric variables, and a "null string" (a string with no characters) to a string variable. **This is your only warning!**

READ

Can you figure out what Line 40 does?

If you guessed "nothing", you are close to right. It leaves a blank line in the printout, thus separating each loop through the program. This is just to keep you from getting confused when RUNning and using the program.

★ Extra for Experts: Add to or modify the program to tell you the cost of the carpet if it costs $8.99 a square yard. Or a table of costs for various prices of carpets.

(Suggestion: don't use CONTROL/C, just let the program loop enough times to reach BASIC's upper limit for handling numbers. Eventually you should get an OVerflow error, and the computer will stop executing the program.)

DO IT

```
NEW

OK
10 LET N=2
20 LET N=N↑2
30 PRINT N;
40 GOTO 20
RUN
   4    16    256    65536    4.29497E+09    1.84468E+19
?OV ERROR IN 20
OK
```

The OVerflow error message. The number got too big even for a computer!

what's all this gobbledegook?

You can see that after the computer got past **65536**, it started printing the results like this: **4.29497E+09**. This is called *floating point notation,* and it is just a shorthand method of expressing very large numbers or very small decimal fractions. Floating point notation has two parts to it:

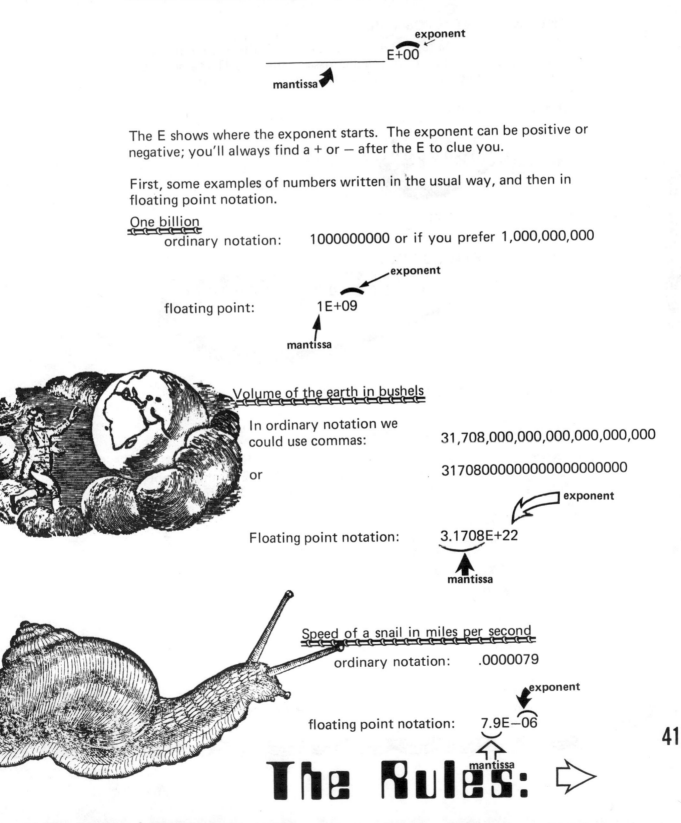

exponent

_____E+00

mantissa

The E shows where the exponent starts. The exponent can be positive or negative; you'll always find a + or − after the E to clue you.

First, some examples of numbers written in the usual way, and then in floating point notation.

One billion

    ordinary notation: 1000000000 or if you prefer 1,000,000,000

exponent

    floating point: 1E+09

mantissa

Volume of the earth in bushels

In ordinary notation we could use commas: 31,708,000,000,000,000,000,000

or   31708000000000000000000

exponent

Floating point notation: 3.1708E+22

mantissa

Speed of a snail in miles per second

    ordinary notation: .0000079

exponent

    floating point notation: 7.9E−06

mantissa

The Rules: ⇨

Floating Point

Now, the rules: how to convert E notation (floating point notation) to ordinary numbers.

IF THE EXPONENT IS POSITIVE:

(1) Write the mantissa separately (that is, leave off the exponent and the E).
(2) Move the decimal point of the mantissa to the RIGHT the number of places specified by the exponent. If necessary, add zeros.

EXAMPLE: 1E+09

$$\overset{1\ 2\ 3\ 4\ 5\ 6\ 7\ 8\ 9}{1.000000000.}$$

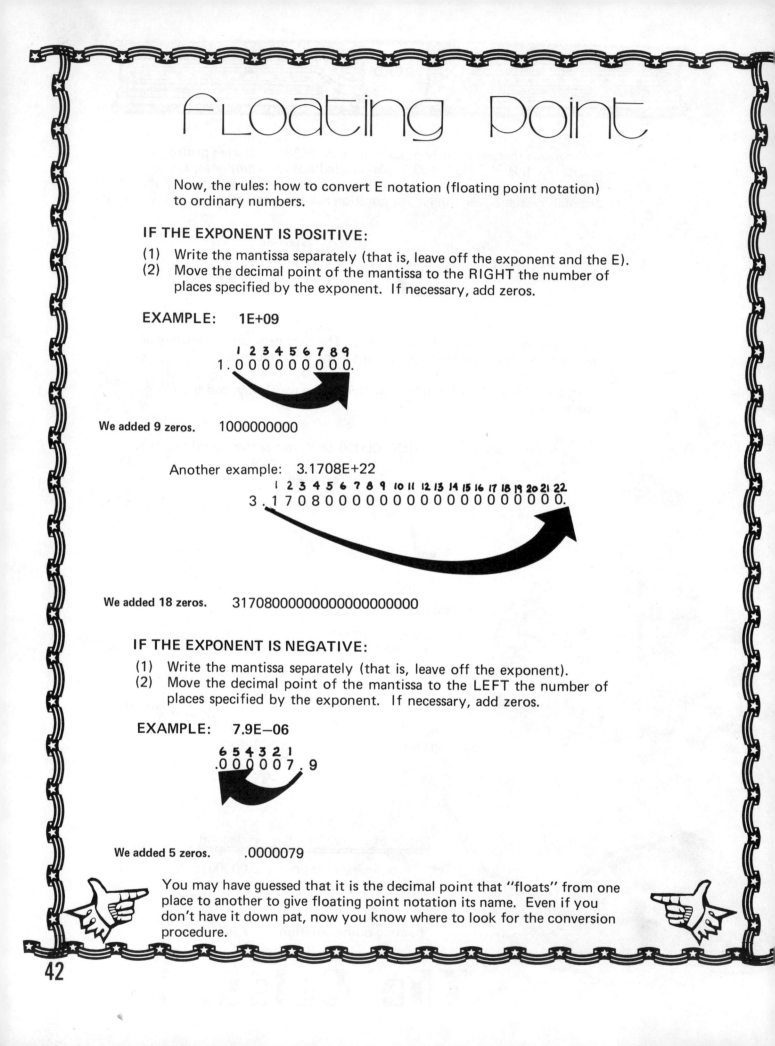

We added 9 zeros. 1000000000

Another example: 3.1708E+22

$$\overset{1\ 2\ 3\ 4\ 5\ 6\ 7\ 8\ 9\ 10\ 11\ 12\ 13\ 14\ 15\ 16\ 17\ 18\ 19\ 20\ 21\ 22}{3.170800000000000000000000.}$$

We added 18 zeros. 31708000000000000000000

IF THE EXPONENT IS NEGATIVE:

(1) Write the mantissa separately (that is, leave off the exponent).
(2) Move the decimal point of the mantissa to the LEFT the number of places specified by the exponent. If necessary, add zeros.

EXAMPLE: 7.9E—06

$$\overset{6\ 5\ 4\ 3\ 2\ 1}{.000007.9}$$

We added 5 zeros. .0000079

You may have guessed that it is the decimal point that "floats" from one place to another to give floating point notation its name. Even if you don't have it down pat, now you know where to look for the conversion procedure.

42

```
NEW

OK
10  PRINT 1000000000000, 123456789, 3.987654321
20  PRINT .000009, .0000000654321, .700007007
30  PRINT 345.3456E4, .3E-9, 6.666666E-4
RUN
  1E+12            1.23457E+08     3.98765
  9E-06            6.54321E-08     .700007
  3.45346E+06      3E-10           6.66667E-04

OK
LIST

10  PRINT 1000000000000, 123456789, 3.987654321
20  PRINT .000009, .0000000654321, .700007007
30  PRINT 345.3456E4, .3E-9, 6.666666E-4
OK
```

So in the future you should understand what happened if the computer gives you a result in E notation.

Have you experimented today?

DO IT HERE! DO IT NOW!

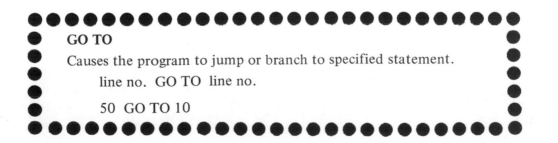

GO TO

Causes the program to jump or branch to specified statement.

　　　line no. GO TO line no.

　　　50 GO TO 10

CHAPTER 3

1. Write these floating point numbers in normal decimal form.

   8.967E5 _____

   1.00E15 _____

   1.0E−3 _____

   6.15762E10 _____

   3.87124E−6 _____

2. Write these decimal numbers in floating point notation.

   1,786,432 _____

   3,134,575,321 _____

   .00012479 _____

   .42456 _____

3. If your program is waiting for data in an INPUT loop (?) and you are OD (out of data), how do you stop the program? _____.

4. If your program is running in an infinite loop — it just keeps on truckin' ... how do you stop it? _____.

5. Write a program to print a table of squares like the one shown below. Program it to go on forever. Stop it when you've had enough.

   ```
   1    1
   2    4
   3    9
   4    16
   5    25
   6    36
   etc.
   ```

6. To help you and your family adjust to the metric system and Celsius temperatures, write a program to prepare a table of Fahrenheit and Celsius temperatures starting at 30 degrees Fahrenheit. (Formula: $C=5/9(F-32)$). Stop the program when you want to.

45

So far, we have been using the simplest possible variables: a letter of the alphabet, or for string variables, a letter followed by the $ that tells the computer to expect a string rather than a numerical value. However, more complicated variables are possible, and sometimes there are good reasons for using them. In a long or complicated program, you may need more than 26 different variables. Or, perhaps for clarity in the program you want to give a variable a label that clearly identifies it, or perhaps you wish a set of related variables to have similar labels.

Rules for variable labels:

The first character of a variable must be a letter of the alphabet. After the first letter, you may use letters, numbers or symbols in the variable name. (A3, A76, AL$, SL$, S3$ etc.)

However, (there's always a however) you may not use as a variable name **or as a part of a variable name**, the words or abbreviations that are actually part of the BASIC language of direct and indirect statements (or functions, which you'll meet later on). Such words as NEW, RUN, INPUT, PRINT or LET are part of the BASIC language and therefore cannot be used as part of variables or data names. For a complete list of reserved (taboo) words that you *can't* use as variable names or part of variable names, see the box below.

Examples of legal variable names:

SALARY	S1
TAX	S2
PLAYER	T%
GUESS	

Examples of no-no's:

LETTER

RUNNY NOSE

LISTERINE

SPRINT

The following is a list of the reserved words in ALTAIR BASIC. You cannot use these words as variable names or as any part of any variable name.

ABS	CLEAR	DATA	DIM	END	FOR	GOSUB
GOTO	IF	INPUT	INT	LET	LIST	NEW	NEXT
PRINT	READ	REM	RESTORE	RETURN	RND
RUN	SGN	SIN	SQR	STEP	STOP	TAB
THEN	TO	USR

ASC	AND	ATN	CHR$	CLOAD	CONT	COS
CSAVE	DEF	EXP	FN	FRE	INPUT	LEFT$	LEN
LOG	MID$	NULL	ON	OR	NOT	OUT	PEEK
POKE	POS	RIGHT$	SPC	STR$	TAN	VAL	WAIT

READ

However, there is a catch in using more than two characters in a variable name: ALTAIR 8K BASIC only looks at the first *two* characters of a variable name. This can lead to interesting results.

DO IT

Try this program using names for variables.

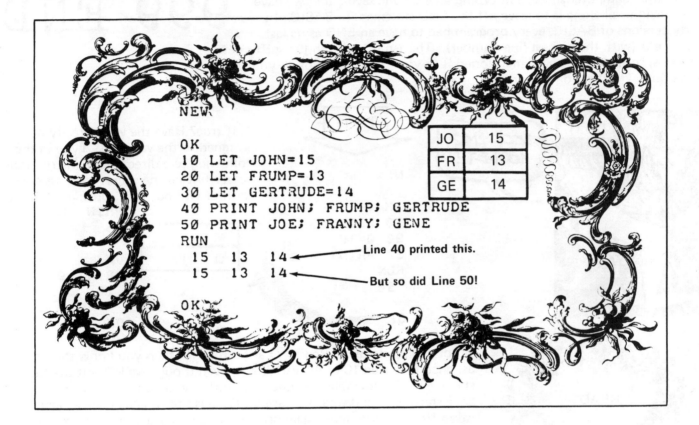

```
NEW

OK
10 LET JOHN=15
20 LET FRUMP=13
30 LET GERTRUDE=14
40 PRINT JOHN; FRUMP; GERTRUDE
50 PRINT JOE; FRANNY; GENE
RUN
   15    13    14  ←——————Line 40 printed this.
   15    13    14  ←——————But so did Line 50!

OK
```

JO	15
FR	13
GE	14

> Yet another good idea, though unfortunately not fully implemented, is the use of datanames. In most high level languages, and assemblers for that matter, one can call a spade a spade. If you are using a variable to store a total you can call it TOTAL. This helps the programmer to remember what goes where. In this BASIC one can call a variable FRAN, if it helps, but you must proceed with considerable caution thereafter. Only the first two letters are checked so any later dataname using the same two will be confused. And you had best not use TOTAL at all. It contains the reserved word TO and any embedded reserved word will cause a syntax error. They are not always easy to spot and MITS BASIC only checks for this at RUN time, a serious weakness in any BASIC and you could find that you have to change every occurrence of a bad dataname. So, if you are starting on a long program, try the proposed dataname first!

Reprinted from the article **Altair BASIC**
by Keith Britton and Bob Mullen,
Peoples Computer Company, *Vol. 4 No. 2*
(Sept. 1975).

Save Time! Save Space!

READ

Before going on to longer programs and more BASIC instructions, here are some time, computer space, and typing savers. One saving that we have been making all along is to leave off the END statement in BASIC. In early versions of BASIC, every program had to have an END as its last statement (with the highest line number). This isn't needed in the spiffy new versions, so we haven't even mentioned it to you. But that's not all you can leave out. Try these demonstration programs.

999 END

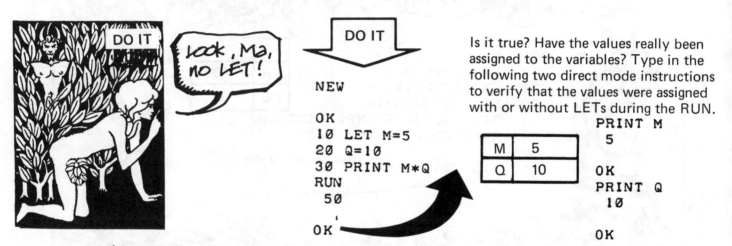

look, Ma, no LET!

DO IT

```
NEW

OK
10 LET M=5
20 Q=10
30 PRINT M*Q
RUN
   50

OK
```

Is it true? Have the values really been assigned to the variables? Type in the following two direct mode instructions to verify that the values were assigned with or without LETs during the RUN.

| M | 5 |
| Q | 10 |

```
PRINT M
5

OK
PRINT Q
10

OK
```

READ

If your computer evaluated M*Q as 5 times 10, then you know that it assigned the value 10 to the variable Q, even though we left out the LET statement. So now that you understand that you don't need a LET in a LET statement, and what you are LETting is the variable Q be assigned the value 10, you need never again use LET in a LET statement. (Now repeat that *verbatim* — yeah, word for word!)

When you use LET, you lose room in the computer's memory, but you gain a little time, faster execution by the computer.

DO IT

Try another LETless statement...

```
NEW

OK
10 G=13
20 PRINT G
RUN
   13

OK
```

| G | 13 |

48

And so, in the name of Efficiency and Ease, the LET was banished forever from Statementland...

Prevent Unsightly Callouses!

But leaving out LET isn't the only shortcut our spiffy new BASIC provides the programmer with callouses on his/her typing fingers. Here's the short form for entering a PRINT statement:?

```
NEW

OK
10 PRINT "HELLO GOOD LOOKING"
20 ? "USING ? FOR PRINT"
RUN
HELLO GOOD LOOKING
USING ? FOR PRINT

OK
```

? means PRINT when entering

Next, LIST the program and note what replaces the question mark in Line 20 of the LISTing.

```
LIST

10 PRINT "HELLO GOOD LOOKING"
20 PRINT "USING ? FOR PRINT"
OK
```

You use ? when you enter the program (saves typing). But when you LIST the program, the smart computer prints PRINT.

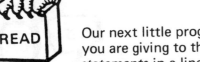

Our next little program shows how you can pack and crunch the instructions you are giving to the computer into fewer statements, by using *multiple statements* in a line.

Use (:) (colon) to separate statements in a multiple statement line.

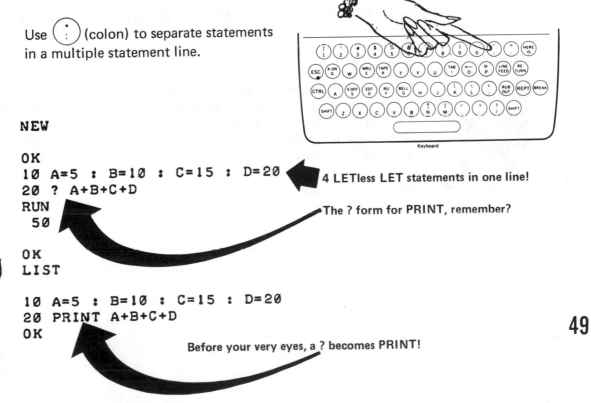

Keyboard

```
NEW

OK
10 A=5 : B=10 : C=15 : D=20
20 ? A+B+C+D
RUN
 50

OK
LIST

10 A=5 : B=10 : C=15 : D=20
20 PRINT A+B+C+D
OK
```

4 LETless LET statements in one line!

The ? form for PRINT, remember?

Well, well, you can put as many statements on a line as will fit, using : to separate the statements.

Before your very eyes, a ? becomes PRINT!

49

DO IT

Same sort of program as on the last page, but all in one multiple statement line!

```
NEW

OK
10 W=2 : X=4 : Y=6 : Z=8 : ? W*X*Y*Z
RUN
 384
```

See the PRINT statement at the end of the line?

```
OK
LIST

10 W=2 : X=4 : Y=6 : Z=8 : PRINT W*X*Y*Z
OK
```

Of course it works for string variables, too!

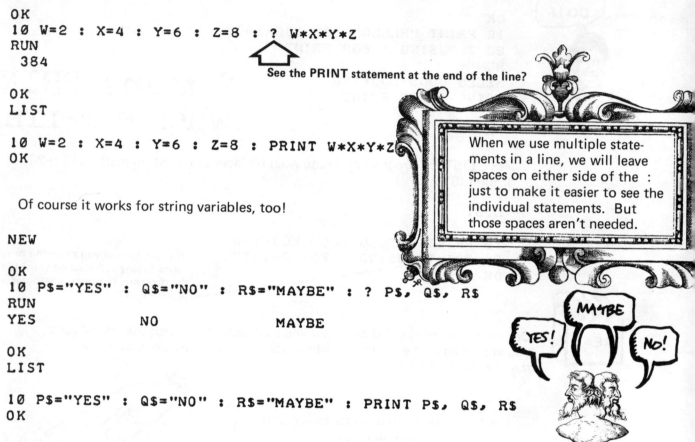

When we use multiple statements in a line, we will leave spaces on either side of the : just to make it easier to see the individual statements. But those spaces aren't needed.

```
NEW

OK
10 P$="YES" : Q$="NO" : R$="MAYBE" : ? P$, Q$, R$
RUN
YES              NO               MAYBE

OK
LIST

10 P$="YES" : Q$="NO" : R$="MAYBE" : PRINT P$, Q$, R$
OK
```

READ

This is rather condensed program writing, and you may wish to write out your programs without multiple statements per line, just to keep things clear. Later you can rewrite a program in more condensed form if computer storage space for your program is a problem (i.e., it's a really long and involved program, or has a lot of strings, or lots of data). Meanwhile, you can save on typing.

But beware, there *are* some restrictions on what can go where in a line with multiple instructions.

A GOTO may *only* be used as the last statement in a multiple statement line, not in the middle somewhere.

DATA statements may not have any other statements before or after DATA, therefore the DATA statement may never be used in a multiple statement line. DATA statements always stand alone.

Make A REMark

Another statement which must stand alone, or else be the *last* statement in a multiple statement line, is the REMark statement.

DO IT

```
NEW

OK
10  REM-SET X EQUAL TO 5  :  X=5
20  ? X
RUN
 0   ◄
OK
```

Computer never sees X = 5, because when it comes to a REMARK, it skips on to the next line in the program automatically.

Since no other value was assigned to X, the computer assumes that X = 0, and therefore, prints 0. Did you know that? An undefined variable equals zero.

```
NEW

OK
10  X=5  :  REM-SET X EQUAL TO 5
20  ? X
RUN
 5
OK
```

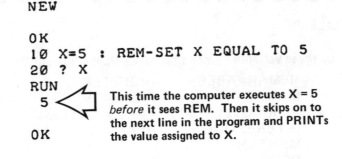

This time the computer executes X = 5 *before* it sees REM. Then it skips on to the next line in the program and PRINTs the value assigned to X.

READ

REMark statements are notes to the person reading a LISTing (or writing!) a program. They are used to explain what that line or section of a program does. REM (for remark) statements are often used to tell where a *subroutine* starts. A subroutine is a section of a program of one or more lines that performs a part of the total job of a program. You'll hear more of subroutines as we get into longer and more complex programs. Meanwhile, if you want to *document* (help explain) your program or tell the reader what your program does, just make a REMark.

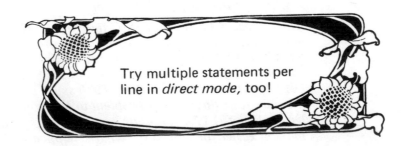

Try multiple statements per line in *direct mode,* too!

REM

Allows comments to be placed in the program. REM is a nonexecutable statement.

line no. REM comments

10 REM THIS PROGRAM WAS DESIGNED BY MJMC
20 REM VARIABLES USED X, Y, Z, A, B, C

BASIC PLUS only

! separates executable portion of line from remarks.

140 LET Z = P*Q ! CALCULATES Z

MULTIPLE STATEMENTS PER LINE

Separated by colon (:).

BASIC PLUS only

Use colon (:) or back slash.

CHAPTER 4   PROBLEMS

1. Circle the part of these variable names that make them "illegal."

CLEARANCE	REMARKABLE	HIGHSTEP
DIMENSION	SINNER	FASINATE
FOREIGN	ABSOLUTELY	FANTABULOUS
CARDIFF	INTERESTING	READABLE
POSITIVE	MANTAN	HOLDOUT
FREEDOM	DEFINATE	GLUCOSE
AMPERSAND	PEEKABOO	

2. In a multiple statement line, DATA statements should only be used

   _____ .

3. In a multiple statement line, GOTO should only be used as the

   _____ .

4. Try redoing Problem 5 from Chapter 3 exercises, as a multiple statement line program.

5. Rewrite two or three of the programs you wrote in previous chapters to take advantage of all these neat, new space and time saving tricks.

SINS OF OMISSION, AND OTHER ERRORS IN MY WAYS —

A word from your friendly author:

All the spaces I leave in BASIC statements are not needed: NO space is needed after the line number, nor after the BASIC statements such as PRINT, READ, DATA, INPUT or other instructions, nor after the items in a PRINT statement (after commas or semicolons). Spaces are NOT needed between DATA statement items either. Each space uses up a little of your computer's memory, but this is not a problem unless your programs are very long or have a lot of DATA values or a lot of strings. I put in those spaces just to make it easier for you to see what is happening in each statement. And rememeber, if you wish to save on typing, you can leave out REMark statements.

52

In Altair BASIC, you do not need to initialize your variables. Initialize means setting your variable values to their first assigned values. If you don't initialize then Altair BASIC automatically assigns a value of zero to a variable the first time that a variable is encountered when the program is RUN. This is an invisible process — that is, it doesn't show in the program itself. If you are sharing your programs with other people, it is considered good programming practice to initialize your variables in the program, rather than letting the computer do it for you. This will avoid confusion to someone else using your program, or even to you if you don't use your program for a while after you first write it.

Refer back to previous explanations and rules of BASIC, for help in writing programs and help in debugging your program if it doesn't RUN without error messages.

You can tell which programs I couldn't type in correctly on one try — they are LISTings with the ? changed to PRINT, with NEW/OK pasted in place at the top. Don't let typing get you down. It's frustrating to get to the end of a complicated multiple statement line and then notice a mistake at the beginning. My frequent errors —

(1)   Forgetting the multiple statement colon, especially after a PRINT statement that ends with a semicolon or comma.

(2)   Forgetting the ? for PRINT, especially in direct mode.

(3)   Using the SHIFT key when I shouldn't, or not using SHIFT when I should.

(4)   Leaving off the quotation marks at the end of a long print line, especially in game program instructions where the sentence doesn't end at the end of the PRINT statement line. You have to type in the whole line over again, just to put the quotation mark at the end.

(5)   Not matching parentheses.

(6)   Another frustrating one is to be entering a statement, but accidently using a line number for a statement you already entered. The first statement with that same line number is replaced by the second one. Double trouble: you must reenter both lines. But stay alert. That SHIFT/@ combination (see page 14) is the one to use to avoid wiping out a previously typed in line (always the most complicated one in the program, of course). But you've got to notice the mistake before you hit RETURN.

It's perfectly alright to break down our multiple statement lines or direct mode instructions into single statements. Since we number our programs by 10's, a three statement line numbered 10, could become lines 10, 11 and 12. You may save time and effort in the long run.

Reminder to users of DEC BASIC PLUS and other versions of BASIC: the printed programs and RUN's in this book were done in Altair 8K BASIC version 3.2. Error messages and other details may be different for the version of BASIC you are using. Check the error message list for your system to avoid confusion. You will probably find the error message list in the appendix of the reference manual for your computer system, unless somebody has removed it ...

In this book we are teaching you how to instruct the computer in BASIC. We are not teaching you how the computer deals with this kind of instruction, or how it performs its "computing" function. If you have more than a passing interest in personal computers, then read YOUR HOME COMPUTER by James White.

Throughout this book we will be showing you some common errors in programming. You learn from mistakes, too, you know. You also learn what the limits are when using BASIC. In addition, you will be familiar with error messages that BASIC provides. These messages give you clues as to the mistakes in your programs, to help you debug them.

compare & decide

Now we come to a very interesting and important capability of BASIC: the ability to compare and decide. In traditional computer jargon, this concept is called *conditional branching*. *Branching* is what happens when the computer follows an instruction that sends it to a different part of the program, *not* in regular line number order. You can think of the GOTO statement as a *branching* statement because it tells the computer to *branch to* and execute a specified statement next, rather than continuing on down the program in line number order.

GO TO _____ (line number) _____

line to branch to

INTRODUCING
IF...THEN

So what we are leading up to is *conditional* branching. If you think about it, you can see that if *branching* means GOTO, then *conditional branching* must mean GOTO, but only under certain conditions. The *condition* is where the computer must compare and decide. Conditions can be true or false. The computer must compare and decide whether a condition is true or false. And now we finally get to the actual BASIC statement that tells the computer to compare and decide: the IF...THEN statement. Actually, there is a whole family of IF...THEN statements. Here is a first look at the IF...THEN statement in its most general form.

Arboreal Branching, not to be confused with Conditional Branching using IF...THEN.

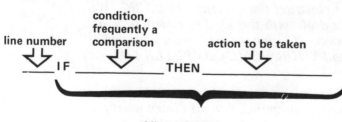

All one BASIC statement

54

ON 1 CONDITION

READ

First warning: if a condition is found to be false, the computer goes on to the next *line numbered statement*. That means that if you use an IF ... THEN statement in a multiple statement line, the computer will not see or execute any other statements following the IF ... THEN statement *if the condition is false*. However, if the condition is true, then the computer will take the action specified following THEN, *and* execute the rest of the statements on the same multiple statement line. As you will see, this fact is actually quite useful.

We told you that there is a whole family of IF...THEN statements. The *condition* (the part between IF and THEN) comes in six different delicious flavors, which you will see in the box on the next page. All of the members of the IF...THEN family of statements can use any one of these six different conditions between IF and THEN. But that isn't what tells the family members apart. The distinction is in what comes after THEN, that is, what action to take *if the condition is true.*

The original IF ... THEN statement, the one that is the most common statement to use for conditional branching, is like having GO TO (line number) after THEN. In fact you can enter it like this:

IF <u>(condition)</u> THEN GO TO <u>(line number)</u>

But even in old fashion BASIC you write it like this, without the GO TO (like leaving out LET in a statement to assign a value to a variable, you know . . .).

IF <u>(condition)</u> THEN <u>(line number)</u>

↑
The GOTO is
understood, but
you don't have
to put it in.

There are two possible outcomes or possible results of the *comparison*. The comparison can be *true*, or it can be *false*. Let's look at these two cases: comparison true, or comparison false.

IF (condition true) THEN (action to take)

Here is where the computer compares and decides that the condition is true.

➡ The computer does what this part tells it to do when the condition is true.

IF (condition false) THEN (action to take)

But if the computer compares and decides that this part is not true (which means it is *false*, of course) ...

⬇ ... then the computer forgets about this part and goes on to the next line numbered statement in the program.

55

6 Possible Conditions
for IF...THEN

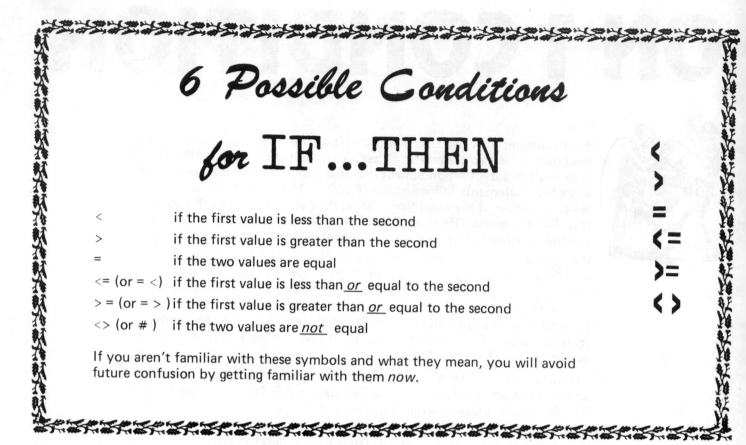

<	if the first value is less than the second
>	if the first value is greater than the second
=	if the two values are equal
<= (or = <)	if the first value is less than _or_ equal to the second
> = (or = >)	if the first value is greater than _or_ equal to the second
<> (or #)	if the two values are _not_ equal

If you aren't familiar with these symbols and what they mean, you will avoid future confusion by getting familiar with them *now.*

IF...THEN PRINT

READ

A second member of the IF...THEN family is the IF...THEN PRINT statement. Instead of having a line number after THEN for the computer to branch or GOTO, you can have the statement PRINT anything a PRINT statement can PRINT, following all the rules for regular PRINT statements. IF...THEN PRINT only PRINTs *if the condition is true,* of course.

IF (condition) THEN PRINT (anything a PRINT statement can do)

If the condition is *false,* then the computer will *not* PRINT anything, and just go right on to the next line numbered statement in the program.

Are you tired of theory and want some action? Are you confused? Don't give up, the light will dawn. For our first demonstration program, let's use IF ... THEN PRINT, only because it will show most clearly how all this comparing and deciding works for you and the computer. We will demonstrate the other IF ... THEN family of statements in due time.

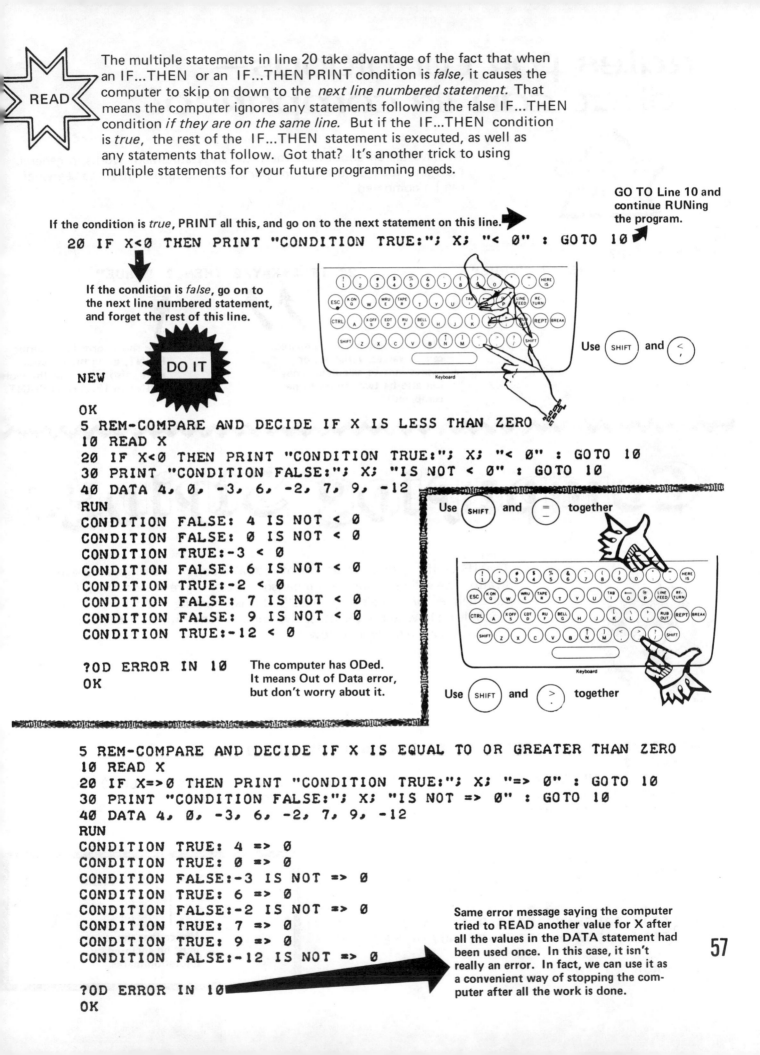
The multiple statements in line 20 take advantage of the fact that when an IF...THEN or an IF...THEN PRINT condition is *false*, it causes the computer to skip on down to the *next line numbered statement*. That means the computer ignores any statements following the false IF...THEN condition *if they are on the same line.* But if the IF...THEN condition is *true*, the rest of the IF...THEN statement is executed, as well as any statements that follow. Got that? It's another trick to using multiple statements for your future programming needs.

GO TO Line 10 and continue RUNing the program.

If the condition is *true*, PRINT all this, and go on to the next statement on this line.

```
20 IF X<Ø THEN PRINT "CONDITION TRUE:"; X; "< Ø" : GOTO 1Ø
```

If the condition is *false*, go on to the next line numbered statement, and forget the rest of this line.

DO IT

NEW

OK
Use SHIFT and <

```
5 REM-COMPARE AND DECIDE IF X IS LESS THAN ZERO
10 READ X
20 IF X<Ø THEN PRINT "CONDITION TRUE:"; X; "< Ø" : GOTO 10
30 PRINT "CONDITION FALSE:"; X; "IS NOT < Ø" : GOTO 10
40 DATA 4, Ø, -3, 6, -2, 7, 9, -12
RUN
CONDITION FALSE: 4 IS NOT < Ø
CONDITION FALSE: Ø IS NOT < Ø
CONDITION TRUE:-3 < Ø
CONDITION FALSE: 6 IS NOT < Ø
CONDITION TRUE:-2 < Ø
CONDITION FALSE: 7 IS NOT < Ø
CONDITION FALSE: 9 IS NOT < Ø
CONDITION TRUE:-12 < Ø

?OD ERROR IN 1Ø
OK
```

Use SHIFT and = together

The computer has ODed. It means Out of Data error, but don't worry about it.

Use SHIFT and > together

```
5 REM-COMPARE AND DECIDE IF X IS EQUAL TO OR GREATER THAN ZERO
10 READ X
20 IF X=>Ø THEN PRINT "CONDITION TRUE:"; X; "=> Ø" : GOTO 10
30 PRINT "CONDITION FALSE:"; X; "IS NOT => Ø" : GOTO 10
40 DATA 4, Ø, -3, 6, -2, 7, 9, -12
RUN
CONDITION TRUE: 4 => Ø
CONDITION TRUE: Ø => Ø
CONDITION FALSE:-3 IS NOT => Ø
CONDITION TRUE: 6 => Ø
CONDITION FALSE:-2 IS NOT => Ø
CONDITION TRUE: 7 => Ø
CONDITION TRUE: 9 => Ø
CONDITION FALSE:-12 IS NOT => Ø

?OD ERROR IN 1Ø
OK
```

Same error message saying the computer tried to READ another value for X after all the values in the DATA statement had been used once. In this case, it isn't really an error. In fact, we can use it as a convenient way of stopping the computer after all the work is done.

57

RULES FOR CONDITIONS — WHAT CAN BE COMPARED?

DO IT

We have talked about how the IF...THEN statement works in general. Now let's look at just the *comparison or condition* itself to see what can be compared.

```
NEW

OK
10 X=5 : Y=20
20 IF 2*X=Y/2 THEN ? "TRUE"
RUN
TRUE

OK
```

```
20 IF 2*X=Y/2 THEN ? "TRUE"
```

The two items to be compared can be values, variables, or expressions to calculate. They can also be two strings to be compared.

The short form for entering PRINT, using the question mark, also works for the word PRINT in IF...THEN PRINT.

Comparing Strings

DO IT

NEW

The IF...THEN family of statements can also compare strings. As a demonstration, we will use a simple comparison: is a string read from the DATA statement *equal to* the string "YES"? If it is, then the comparison is *true*. You'll learn how to use the other five comparisons with strings later on. For now, try the program below.

```
OK
5 REM-COMPARE AND DECIDE IF X$ STRING IS EQUAL TO "YES"
10 READ X$
20 IF X$="YES" THEN PRINT "CONDITION TRUE:"; X$; " = YES" : GOTO 10
30 PRINT "CONDITION FALSE:"; X$; " DOES NOT = YES" : GOTO 10
40 DATA YES, NO, MAYBE, YES, NO, MAYBE

RUN
CONDITION TRUE:YES = YES
CONDITION FALSE:NO DOES NOT = YES
CONDITION FALSE:MAYBE DOES NOT = YES
CONDITION TRUE:YES = YES
CONDITION FALSE:NO DOES NOT = YES
CONDITION FALSE:MAYBE DOES NOT = YES

?OD ERROR IN 10
OK
```

58

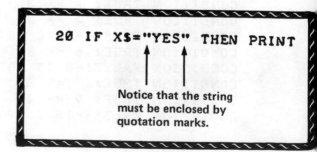

```
20 IF X$="YES" THEN PRINT
```

Notice that the string must be enclosed by quotation marks.

TEST AND DECIDE

The next program has three IF...THEN PRINT statements to test the same value up to three times. There are three different conditions to test Notice the multiple statements in lines 20, 30, and 40. When the IF... THEN PRINT condition is *false,* the computer skips to the next *line numbered statement*, and ignores any other statements following the false IF...THEN on the same line. But if the IF...THEN PRINT condition is *true*, then the rest of the IF...THEN PRINT statement is executed, *as well as any statements that follow it on the same line.*

IF ... THEN ? = IF ... THEN PRINT

```
NEW

OK
5 REM- NEGATIVE, POSITIVE AND ZERO NUMBER TESTER
10 INPUT "INPUT 0 (ZERO) OR ANY NEGATIVE OR POSITIVE NUMBER"; N
20 IF N<0 THEN ? "YOUR NUMBER IS NEGATIVE." : ? : GOTO10
30 IF N>0 THEN ? "YOUR NUMBER IS POSITIVE." : ? : GOTO 10
40 IF N=0 THEN ? "YOUR NUMBER IS ZERO." : ? : GOTO 10
RUN
INPUT 0 (ZERO) OR ANY NEGATIVE OR POSITIVE NUMBER? 8975
YOUR NUMBER IS POSITIVE.

INPUT 0 (ZERO) OR ANY NEGATIVE OR POSITIVE NUMBER? -384
YOUR NUMBER IS NEGATIVE.

INPUT 0 (ZERO) OR ANY NEGATIVE OR POSITIVE NUMBER? 0
YOUR NUMBER IS ZERO.

INPUT 0 (ZERO) OR ANY NEGATIVE OR POSITIVE NUMBER?

OK
```

Let's take a closer look at one of the IF ... THEN PRINT statements.

PRINT a blank line (between loops in the RUN).

If the condition is *true*, PRINT the string, and go on to the next statement.

```
20 IF N<0 THEN ? "YOUR NUMBER IS NEGATIVE." : ? : GOTO 10
```

If the condition is *false*, go on to the next line numbered statement, and forget the rest of this line. That means don't do anything following THEN.

GOTO line 10 and continue RUNning the program.

WHAT IS A FILTER?

FOR STRAINING: Muslin, or nylon sieve

The next program is similar to the last one. However, notice that the conditions tested are comparisons of the two INPUT values X and Y. This sort of subroutine is used in many programs to check for various things (make several comparisons) about data or inputs. It's almost a game program.

DO IT

```
NEW

OK
5 REM-COMPARISON OR "FILTER" PROGRAM
10 INPUT "INPUT ANY TWO NUMBERS"; Y,Z
20 IF Y<Z THEN ? Y; "IS LESS THAN "; Z
30 IF Y>Z THEN ? Y; "IS GREATER THAN "; Z
40 IF Y=Z THEN ? Y; "IS EQUAL TO "; Z
50 ?
60 GOTO 10
RUN
INPUT ANY TWO NUMBERS? 8,53
 8 IS LESS THAN  53

INPUT ANY TWO NUMBERS? 2001,1999
 2001 IS GREATER THAN  1999

INPUT ANY TWO NUMBERS? -12,-33
-12 IS GREATER THAN -33

INPUT ANY TWO NUMBERS? 81,81
 81 IS EQUAL TO  81

INPUT ANY TWO NUMBERS?

OK
```

We have the computer ask for two values, and to assign one to Y and the other for Z.

PRINTs nothing, leaving a blank line between loops.

The INPUTs must be separated with a comma.

Correction with ← is OK when entering an INPUT, but once you've pressed RETURN...

Hit RETURN to stop the RUN of a program waiting for an INPUT. If that doesn't work, try CONTROL/C.

READ

After the INPUT question mark, did you remember to separate your INPUT values with a comma?

Note that the computer compares the values of Y and Z three times, whether it has to or not. Compare this with the NEG, POS, ZERO NUMBER TESTER.

In the filter (it filters through the possibilities, get it?) part of the program (Lines 20, 30 and 40), the computer only does what the IF statement says to do (PRINT) if the comparison is *true*.

To Print or Not To Print:
That is the Question

Now please pay close attention to these next little programs using the IF...THEN statement. Line 20 is used to decide whether to PRINT a value or not. When the condition is *false*, the computer skips on to the line 30 PRINT statement and PRINTs the value of R. But when the condition is *true*, the computer *branches* back to line 10. It does not get to line 30, and therefore it doesn't PRINT. Instead, a new value is assigned to R from the DATA. Then the new value is tested by line 20. And so on.

At first, this may seem backwards to you. Just remember that the action indicated after THEN only happens *if the condition is true.* Now go ahead and try the programs.

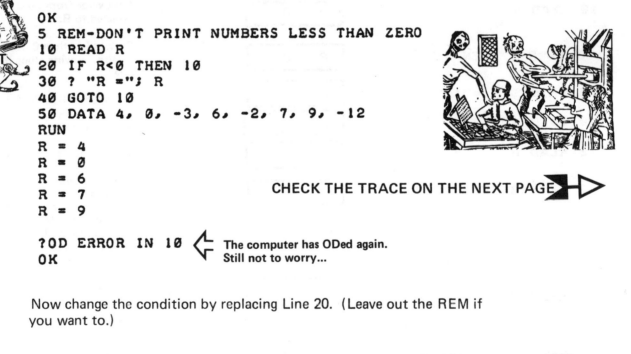

```
NEW

OK
5 REM-DON'T PRINT NUMBERS LESS THAN ZERO
10 READ R
20 IF R<0 THEN 10
30 ? "R ="; R
40 GOTO 10
50 DATA 4, 0, -3, 6, -2, 7, 9, -12
RUN
R = 4
R = 0
R = 6
R = 7
R = 9

?OD ERROR IN 10
OK
```

CHECK THE TRACE ON THE NEXT PAGE ⟿

⟵ The computer has ODed again.
Still not to worry...

Now change the condition by replacing Line 20. (Leave out the REM if you want to.)

```
5 REM-DON'T PRINT NUMBERS GREATER THAN ZERO
20 IF R>0 THEN 10
RUN
R = 0
R =-3
R =-2
R =-12

?OD ERROR IN 10
OK
```

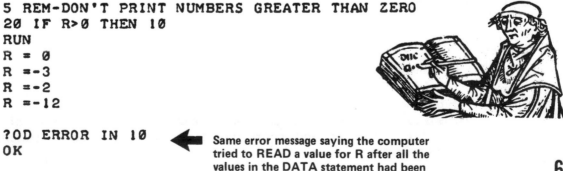

⟵ Same error message saying the computer tried to READ a value for R after all the values in the DATA statement had been used once.

TRACE FOR CONDITIONAL BRANCHING

Below is a trace for part of the RUN for the first IF...THEN example program on the last page. The condition tested is R < 0 (R less than 0). The effect is "Don't Print Numbers Less Than Zero." Go through this trace to see the decisions made by the computer: To Print or Not To Print.

STATEMENT	VARIABLES & VALUES	DESCRIPTION
5 REM-DON'T PRINT NUMBERS LESS THAN ZERO		The computer skips REMarks.
10 READ R	R 4	First item from Line 50 DATA is assigned to READ variable R.
20 IF R<0 THEN 10	R 4	The computer compares the value in R to 0 (zero). Since 4 is *not* less than 0, the condition is false and the computer goes on to the next line.
30 PRINT "R ="; R	R 4	Value of R is PRINTed.
40 GOTO 10	R 4	Computer goes back to Line 10.
10 READ R	R 0	Next value from 50 DATA assigned to R.
20 IF R<0 THEN 10	R 0	0 is *not* less than 0, so the condition is false. Moving along to the next line ...
30 PRINT "R ="; R	R 0	the value of R is PRINTed.
40 GOTO 10	R 0	And back we go to Line 10 ...
10 READ R	R −3	Third item from 50 DATA.
20 IF R<0 THEN 10	R −3	Well, this time the value of R = −3, which is *less* than 0 (the condition is true) so the computer follows the rest of the IF ... THEN statement instructions, and loops back to Line 10, skipping the PRINT statement in Line 30, etc.
10 READ R	R 6	New value for R.
50 DATA 4, 0, -3, 6, -2, 7, 9, -12		Line 10 READs DATA from line 50.

Technically, this process is called *conditional branching*. If a condition is true, the computer branches to another part of the program.

IF the condition is *true*, the computer does what the rest of the statement tells it to. But IF the condition is *false*, the computer ignores the rest of the IF ... THEN statement and goes right on to the next line numbered statement in the program.

stop the loop!

This is the condition

Line number

Do what this says if the condition is *true*. In this case, go to the statement with this line number.

```
30 IF T<10 THEN 10
```

DO IT

Go on to the next line numbered statement if the condition is *false*.

That means go to the next statement with the smallest line number greater than 30.

Now enter and RUN this program to stop a loop after a certain number of times, using the IF...THEN statement to do the checking.

```
NEW

OK
5 REM-SELF-STOPPING COUNTING PROGRAM
10 ? T
20 T=T+1
30 IF T<10 THEN 10
40 ? "NOW T ="; T; "SO I STOPPED MYSELF."
RUN
 0
 1
 2
 3
 4
 5
 6
 7
 8
 9
NOW T = 10 SO I STOPPED MYSELF.

OK
```

READ

Our IF statement (Line 30 above) asks the profound question, "Is the value of T less than 10?" When the answer is "true," THEN 10 tells the computer to branch or loop back to Line 10. But when the answer to the profound question is "no" (when the value of T finally reaches 10), the computer ignores the rest of the IF statement and "falls through" to the next line in the program (Line 40).

63

IF THEN
(IF GOTO)

Causes program to jump or branch if the relation is true. Otherwise the program continues to next line numbered statement.

line no. IF (condition) THEN (line no.) or statement

```
10  IF X  10 THEN 50
10  IF X  10 THEN PRINT "NUMBER IS LESS THAN 10"
10  IF X 10 THEN PRINT "ERROR" : X = 0 : GO TO 50
10  IF A$ = "YES" THEN PRINT "GOODBYE FOR NOW" : END
```

IF GOTO is acceptable but must be followed by a line number.

THE IF...THEN FAMILY

IF...THEN (GOTO)   the GOTO may be omitted
IF...THEN PRINT or IF...THEN ?
IF...THEN (LET)   the LET may be omitted
IF...THEN INPUT
IF...THEN READ
IF...THEN GOSUB
IF...THEN RETURN
IF...THEN STOP
IF...THEN END

BASIC PLUS only

BASIC PLUS has == which means "approximately = to."

64

1. In an IF-THEN statement, if the condition is FALSE the program
   _____.

2. In the statement IF X <> THEN 100, the test is to see if the two
   variables are _____.

3. IF X <= Y THEN 100 is testing to see if the value of X is _____
   the value of Y.

4. Here is a program to search through a data list and print all the numbers
   over 100. What is wrong with the program?

   ```
   10  READ A
   20  IF A > 100 THEN 30
   30  GOTO 10
   40  DATA 12, 112, 30, 230, 400, 24
   ```

5. Compute your water bill! Remember Problem 8 at the end of Chapter 2?
   You attempted to compute your water usage for the month in gallons.
   Now for the bad news, the bill.

   Assume everyone pays a meter fee of $2.85 per month and that water is
   billed by the cubic foot (remember: 7.5 gallons per cubic foot).

   Write a program to compute your water bill if you are charged $0.50 per
   100 cubic feet used. Enter usage in gallons (don't forget to add the meter
   fee). For 6000 gallons the answer is $6.85.   10,000 gallons = $9.52
   and 20,000 gallons = $16.18.

6. Using the data from Problem 5 above, let's assume the water company
   starts to penalize large users by charging more for water used in excess
   of some 'normal' amount. Let's assume a family of four is allowed
   8000 gallons per month and is charged $0.50 per 100 cubic feet for
   those 8000 gallons (plus the meter fee). For any gallonage over 8000,
   the charge is $1.00 per 100 cubic feet. Write a program to compute the
   water bill under this system (it could happen . . .).

7. Sell computer time to a neighbor . . . for fun and profit! You'll need
   a timeclock of some sort and a computer program to do the calculations.
   Charge $2.00 just for the privilege of using the system plus $0.05 per
   minute for the first 45 minutes and $0.03 per 100 minutes used.

   $$45 \times .05 = 2.25$$
   $$(100 - 45) \times .03 = 1.65$$
   $$\text{connect fee} = 2.00$$

   Total = $5.90

   Tip: What if the user uses less than 45 minutes. Don't forget to 'program'
   for that possibility.

8. String comparisons: You have a huge customer list of 4000 names
   contained in DATA statements with names and zip coded expressions
   in two different strings. (Why did we place zip codes in string variables
   instead of numbers?)

   DATA LISA STEWART, 94061

   You are about to travel to zip code area 94061. Read through the names in
   your DATA statements and select and print only those names in zip
   area 94061 so you will know whom to call on while you are in the area.

FUNCTION JUNCTION #1

BASIC includes some "automatic" features called *functions*. Sometimes these *functions* are like formulas or equations for doing certain kinds of things to numbers or strings. A complete list of functions is on page 158.

Our first BASIC function is the SQR(x) function. This is the SQuare Root function. It tells the computer to find the *square root* of whatever value is enclosed in the parentheses.

SQUARES AND SQUARE ROOTS EXPLAINED

The *square* of a number is that number multiplied by itself. For example,

9 time 9 = 81   Same as 9^2 (nine squared) or 9↑2 in BASIC

81 is the *square* of 9.

It works the other way too. The *square root* of a number is another number which, multiplied by itself, gives the first number. For example, 9 is a square root of 81 because 9*9 = 81. In math books they write it like this:

$$\sqrt{81} = 9$$

—9 is also a square root of 81 because (—9)*(—9) = 81. However, BASIC only computes the non-negative square root.

The square root of 9 is 3 because 3 times 3 equals 9.

You can only find the SQR of positive numbers, not negative numbers.

As you will see, the square root of a number is not usually a whole number like 3, but is more often a number with a decimal fraction.

66

Use direct mode to experiment with the SQR(X) function. Try the examples below *and* try your own ideas.

```
PRINT SQR(100)
 10

OK
```

A variable, a value, or an expression to calculate.

```
? SQR(85)
 9.21955

OK
? SQR(1), SQR(2), SQR(3), SQR(4)
 1             1.41421        1.73205         2

OK
? SQR(5); SQR(6); SQR(7); SQR(8); SQR(9); SQR(10)
 2.23607  2.44949  2.64575  2.82843  3  3.16228

OK
```

Now, still using direct mode, try to make BASIC find the SQR of a negative number.

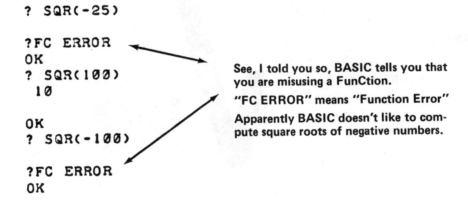

```
? SQR(-25)

?FC ERROR
OK
? SQR(100)
 10

OK
? SQR(-100)

?FC ERROR
OK
```

See, I told you so, BASIC tells you that you are misusing a FunCtion.

"FC ERROR" means "Function Error"

Apparently BASIC doesn't like to compute square roots of negative numbers.

Next, try some calculations that include the SQR function.

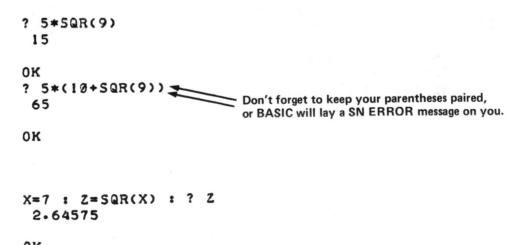

```
? 5*SQR(9)
 15

OK
? 5*(10+SQR(9))
 65

OK
```

Don't forget to keep your parentheses paired, or BASIC will lay a SN ERROR message on you.

```
X=7 : Z=SQR(X) : ? Z
 2.64575

OK
```

Do your own experimenting, and then try these programs.

```
NEW

OK
10 X=7
20 Z=SQR(X)
30 ? Z
RUN
 2.64575

OK
```

```
NEW

OK
10 INPUT A
20 ? A; SQR(A)
30 ? : GOTO 10
RUN
? 225
  225  15

? 33
  33  5.74456

?
OK
```

Did you hit RETURN?

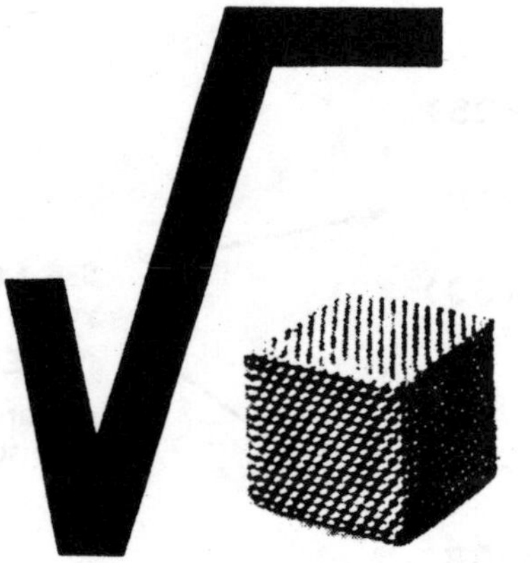

```
NEW

OK
5 REM-SQUARE ROOT MACHINE
10 ? "GIVE ME A NUMBER AND I WILL TELL YOU THE SQUARE ROOT."
20 INPUT "NUMBER PLEASE"; A
30 ? "THE SQUARE ROOT OF"; A; "IS"; SQR(A) : ? : GOTO20
RUN
GIVE ME A NUMBER AND I WILL TELL YOU THE SQUARE ROOT.
NUMBER PLEASE? 7
THE SQUARE ROOT OF 7 IS 2.64575

NUMBER PLEASE? 1444
THE SQUARE ROOT OF 1444 IS 38

NUMBER PLEASE?

OK
```

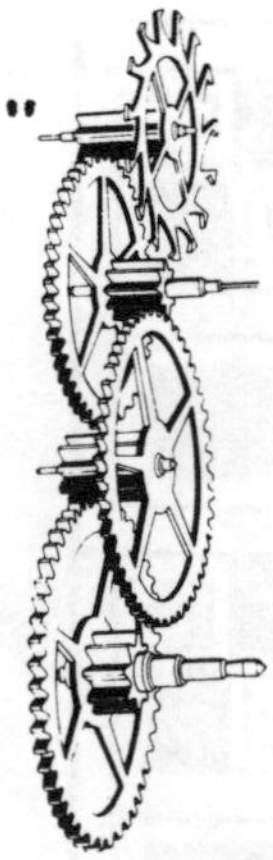

68

 **INT( )** A variable, a value, or an expression to calculate.

READ

INT(X)   tells the computer to find the *integer* part of a positive number. The *integer* part of a number is the whole number part without the decimal fraction, like this:

INT(5.6) = 5   The integer part of 5.6 is 5.

Find the integer part of the numbers in the INT parentheses, using direct mode.

DO IT

```
? INT(3.1)
 3

OK
? INT(3.9999), INT(101.1), INT(3.14159)
 3              101           3

OK
```

Now try negative numbers. The INT function returns the next more negative integer. INT(−5.6) = −6. The integer part of −5.6 is −6.

```
? INT(5.1), INT(-5.1), INT(5.9999), INT(-5.9999)
 5           -6          5            -6

OK
```

See the difference in the way the INT works with a negative number as compared to a positive number?

Find the integer part of the square root of 52.

```
? SQR(52), INT(SQR(52))
 7.2111        7

OK
```

Note the clever use of a function inside the parentheses of another function. Again BASIC starts on the inner most set of parentheses and works out. Don't forget to match each left parentheses with a right parentheses.

fraction chopper offer

INT

69

ROUNDING OFF USING INT

It is often convenient to *round off* a calculation, rather than just chopping off the decimal fraction. *Rounding off* a number means that the number becomes the integer part if the decimal fraction is less than .5 (one half), that is, 5.4 becomes 5.

If the decimal fraction part of the number is .5 or greater, then the number is rounded off to the next *higher* integer, that is, 5.6 rounds off to 6.

Here is how you use the INT function to round off a number.

INT(X + .5)   INT(5.4 + .5) = 5   (5.9 without the .9)

INT(5.6 + .5) = 6   (6.1 without the .1)

RUN this program to round off the positive numbers in the DATA statement.

DO IT

```
NEW

OK
5 REM-NUMBER ROUNDER OFFER
10 READ X : ? X, INT(X+.5) : GOTO 10
20 DATA 3.14159, 101.888, 521.999, 521.001, 521.5
RUN
   3.14159        3
   101.888        102
   521.999        522
   521.001        521
   521.5          522

?OD ERROR IN 10
OK
```
◄ Don't worry, it's just the Out of Data message.

ROUNDING OFF MONEY

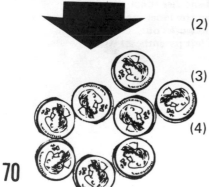

The example problem: Calculate the sales tax on an item that cost $17.95 and the tax rate is 6%. Round off the results to the nearest whole penny.

$17.95 x .06 = $1.077

(1) Multiply the amount to be rounded off by 100. This moves the decimal point two place to the right.

1.077 x 100 = 107.7

(2) Add .5 to the number, as the rounder offer.

107.7 + .5 = 108.2

(3) Take the integer part of this value.

INT(108.2) = 108

(4) Divide by 100 to move the decimal point back to its original position, two places to the left.

108/100 = 1.08, so we have $1.08 as the sales tax on $17.95, rounded off to the nearest whole penny.

Now let's have the computer do the problem. Note that we instruct the computer to PRINT the value of M after each step of the rounding off process, just to help us see how the process works step-by-step.

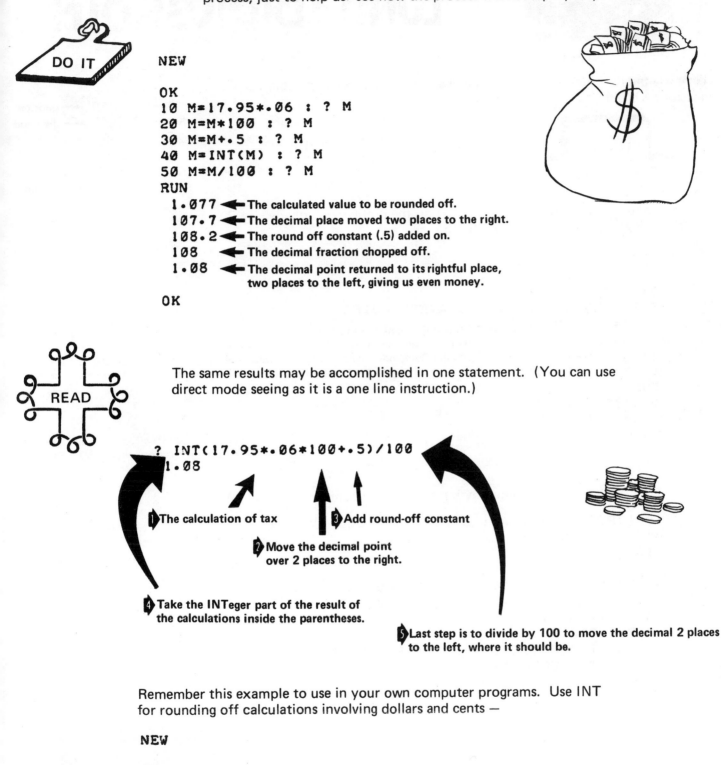

```
NEW

OK
10 M=17.95*.06 : ? M
20 M=M*100 : ? M
30 M=M+.5 : ? M
40 M=INT(M) : ? M
50 M=M/100 : ? M
RUN
   1.077  ◄── The calculated value to be rounded off.
   107.7  ◄── The decimal place moved two places to the right.
   108.2  ◄── The round off constant (.5) added on.
   108    ◄── The decimal fraction chopped off.
   1.08   ◄── The decimal point returned to its rightful place,
              two places to the left, giving us even money.
OK
```

The same results may be accomplished in one statement. (You can use direct mode seeing as it is a one line instruction.)

```
? INT(17.95*.06*100+.5)/100
1.08
```

1 The calculation of tax

3 Add round-off constant

2 Move the decimal point over 2 places to the right.

4 Take the INTeger part of the result of the calculations inside the parentheses.

5 Last step is to divide by 100 to move the decimal 2 places to the left, where it should be.

Remember this example to use in your own computer programs. Use INT for rounding off calculations involving dollars and cents —

```
NEW

OK
10 M=17.95*.06
20 ? INT(M*100+.5)/100
RUN
   1.08
```

M can be the result of calculations, or it can be a value calculated earlier in the program.

READ

Let's use the INT function to do "long division" problems. Remember long division? Or did you learn new math?

DO IT

```
                    19  ← quotient
divisor →  5 )97  ← dividend
               5
               47
               45
                2  ← remainder
```

Now get the computer to do it for you. First, the problem: A divided by B, A/B (or B)A) where A = 97 and B = 5.

```
NEW

OK
5 REM-LONG DIVISION CRANKER OUTER
10 A=97 : B=5 ←Values of A and B assigned in this line.
20 Q=INT(A/B) ←The Quotient: the number of complete times B goes into A (5 goes into 97).†
30 R=A-B*Q   ← Line 30 gets the Remainder: what's left over from A when you divide by B. 97—(5*19).
40 ? "QUOTIENT ="; Q : ? "REMAINDER ="; R    Did you notice the neat way we did this?
RUN
QUOTIENT = 19
REMAINDER = 2


OK
```

† Note: Line 20 actually calculates the result with a decimal fraction, which INT chops off.

Try it with your own values, by replacing Line 10 and adding Line 60.

```
10 INPUT "A ="; A : INPUT "DIVIDED BY"; B
60 ? : GOTO 10
LIST

5 REM-LONG DIVISION CRANKER OUTER
10 INPUT "A ="; A : INPUT "DIVIDED BY"; B
20 Q=INT(A/B)
30 R=A-B*Q
40 PRINT "QUOTIENT ="; Q : PRINT "REMAINDER ="; R
60 PRINT : GOTO 10
OK
RUN
A =? 97
DIVIDED BY? 5
QUOTIENT = 19
REMAINDER = 2

A =? 2435
DIVIDED BY? 14
QUOTIENT = 173
REMAINDER = 13

A =?

OK
```

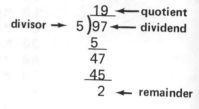

The third function we want you to learn is the RND(x) function. *Random* means that something happens just by chance. It's like picking numbers out of a hat. The RND function is tricky. When you instruct the computer with the RND function, it gives you a *random* number (that looks like a decimal fraction) between zero and one. Never 0, never 1, always *between*, my friend. If the RND number (the decimal fraction is very small, that is, very close to zero, it may be printed in floating point notation. The number, variable or calculation found in the parentheses of these functions is often referred to as the expression or *argument* for the function . . . wanna fight about it? There are three types of *arguments* that may be used in the parentheses for the RND(X) function, for three different effects. Do the following exercises and you will see how RND works.

DO IT

RND(1)

RND argument is positive.

```
NEW

OK
10 X=1
20 ? RND(X) : GOTO 20
RUN
 .50438
 .0267824
 .388094
 .569123
 .720021
 .209046
 .599886

BREAK IN 20
OK
```

Don't expect the RND numbers for your RUN to be the same as these. After all, they are supposed to be "random."

This happened because we pressed CONTROL/C.

Now RUN the program again, and compare the RND numbers from this RUN with the RND numbers from the first RUN.

```
RUN
 .744055
 .460434
 .433291
 .27376
 .701146
 .590584
 .457448

BREAK IN 20
OK
```

Note that the RND numbers from this RUN of the same program are different.

RND(0)

Zero for the RND argument.

Now replace line 10 with this new line 10, and after a few sample RND numbers, stop with CONTROL/C.

```
10 X=0
RUN
 .457448
 .457448
 .457448
 .457448
 .457448
 .457448
 .457448

BREAK IN 20
OK
```

Note this RND number, then look back at the last RND number in the previous RUN. Interesting, eh?

Now RUN again, then stop the execution with CONTROL/C and compare with the previous RUNs.

```
RUN
 .457448
 .457448
 .457448

BREAK IN 20
OK
```

RND(-1)

RND argument is negative.

Replace line 10 again, like this:

```
10 X=-.4
RUN
 .803906
 .803906
 .803906

BREAK IN 20
OK
```

Again, stop with CONTROL/C, do another RUN, and compare it with the others.

```
RUN
 .803906
 .803906

BREAK IN 20
OK
```

Another negative value for X.

```
10 X=-1
RUN
 7.65943E-06
 7.65943E-06
 7.65943E-06
 7.65943E-06

BREAK IN 20
OK
```

A "small" RND number (close to zero) is printed in floating point notation.

And yet another negative value.

```
10 X=-.3
RUN
 .905996
 .905996

BREAK IN 20
OK
```

Hmmm...confused? Perplexed? Read on & all will be revealed.

73

My dear Watson, we may now begin to deduce from these experiments just what the rules are for getting what you want from the RND function.

RND ARGUMENT IS POSITIVE

For a new and different RND number every time the computer executes a statement with a RND function, the number in the parentheses must be greater than zero (any positive number). You may use *any* positive number as the argument, such as 1, which you used in the first RND demo program on the last page.

You can use decimal fractions, or numbers with decimal fractions, such as RND(3.52), but it doesn't matter as far as getting a new RND number each time a statement with RND is executed.

This type of RND function is useful in game-playing programs, where you want an element of chance.

RND ARGUMENT IS ZERO

Using 0 as the argument gets you the same RND number repeated over and over again. However, if you look closely at the RUN's, you will see that the RND number you get using 0 as the argument is the *same* as the *last* RND number that was *generated* by RND. *Generated* means produced by the computer from executing the function.

This type of RND function is sometimes useful to debug a program, when you don't want the last RND number generated by the program to change. That way you can see the effect of other variables or values in the program while the RND number stays the same.

Use direct mode to see how RND(0) takes the last RND number generated as its value.

```
? RND(1); RND(0); RND(2); RND(0); RND(-1); RND(0); RND(-.15); RND(0)
 .163989  .163989  .737525  .737525  7.65943E-06  7.65943E-06  .603906
 .603906

OK
```

Try your own values in the non-zero arguments, if you wish.

READf

READ

RND ARGUMENT IS NEGATIVE

Using a negative number as the RND argument also gives you a repeated RND number each time the same RND statement is executed. However, for each different negative argument, you get a different repeated RND number. You can use decimal fractions as the negative arguments, too, such as RND(−.3) or RND(−9.32). Everytime you RUN the program or execute a statement with the *same* negative argument, you get the same RND number.

Demonstrate how RND works with negative arguments, using direct mode.

```
? RND(1); RND(-.4); RND(-.4); RND(-.4); RND(-17.5); RND(-990)
 .905996   .803906   .803906   .803906   8.37562E-06  1.96788E-03

OK
```

Try you own demo with your own choice of RND arguments.

READ

In some cases, it is useful to have the same list of RND numbers used in a program every time that program is RUN. This might be the case for some *simulation* programs. (You'll hear more about simulations later on.) In effect, the RND(−.3) gives the computer an initial RND number to start off the list, and the RND(1) picks up from there and keeps generating more RND numbers. Try our list repeater program.

DO IT

```
NEW

OK
5 REM-RND NUMBER LIST REPEATER
10 X=RND(-.3)
20 ? RND(1)
30 GOTO 20
RUN
 .905996
 .270418
 .504185
 .885868
 .22101
 .457995
```

Use CONTROL/C to stop the RUN.

```
BREAK IN 20
OK
RUN        New RUN, same list.
 .905996
 .270418
 .504185
 .885868
 .22101
 .457995

BREAK IN 20
OK
```

75

RND Integers

But it isn't always handy to have random numbers that are weird decimal fractions between 0 and 1. Let's say we want random numbers between 0 and 9. By a clever combination of the RND and INT functions, we can get BASIC to give us random whole numbers.

```
NEW

OK
5 REM-RND INTEGERS
10 X=RND(1)    ← The RND number is generated and assigned to variable X.
20 X=X*10      ← The RND number multiplied by 10, which moves the decimal point one place to the right.
30 X=INT(X)    ← INT chops off the unwanted fraction, producing a RND integer.
40 ? X;
50 GOTO 10
RUN
 9  1  3  5  5  7  3  8  7  8  5  8  8  4  3  5  2  4  2  4  3  3  4  4
 7  7  5  2  9  1  4  2  9  5  1  8  0  5  6  4  2  0  3  9  7  1  7  3
 0  8  1  9  7  5  0  1  8  6  6  4  1  6  2  2  7
BREAK IN 40
OK
```

Now enter this modified version of the program. It prints headings, and the steps in producing a series of RND integers.

```
NEW

OK
5 REM-RND INTEGERS EXPLAINED
10 ? " X=RND(1)", " X=X*10", " X=INT(X)"
20 X=RND(1) : ? X,
30 X=X*10 : ? X,
40 X=INT(X) : ? X
50 GOTO 20
RUN
```

Which line of the program prints which column of values?

```
 X=RND(1)        X=X*10        X=INT(X)
 .743459         7.43459       7
 .835007         8.35007       8
 .0717177        .717177       0
 .371099         3.71099       3
 .271622         2.71622       2
 .929463         9.29463       9
 .232348
BREAK IN 20
OK
```

RANDOM

How about if we want RND numbers from 1 to 10 instead of from 0 to 9.?
Simple - just add 1 to the value of X. This could be done anytime after the
RND number is generated. Modify the program RND INTEGERS EXPLAINED
by replacing line 10, the headings, changing line 40 to add a comma to the
end of the line, and insert the new line between lines 40 and 50.

```
10 ? " X=RND(1)", " X=X*10", " X=INT(X)", " X=X+1"
40 X=INT(X) : ? X,
45 X=X+1 : ? X
```

You do a LISTing to see the modified program. It should RUN like this:

```
RUN
  X=RND(1)          X=X*10          X=INT(X)          X=X+1
  .951037           9.51037         9                 10
  .376529           3.76529         3                 4
  .220719           2.20719         2                 3
  .379046           3.79046         3                 4
  .818024           8.18024         8                 9
  .989366           9.89366         9                 10
  5.23684E-03       .0523684        0                 1
  .281303           2.81303         2                 3

BREAK IN 45
OK
```

★★

Or get real fancy and do it in one line like this:

```
NEW

OK
10 ? INT(10*RND(1))+1; : GOTO 10
RUN
  9  1  8  1  2  5  7  1  2  6  6  5  9  2  8  10  5  8  2  8  9  6
  7  1  6  7  6  9  10  3  7  8  5  6  1  8  10
BREAK IN 10
OK
RUN
```

Keep your parentheses paired!

Now why do you suppose that semicolon is there?

New RUN, new list of RND integers between 1 and 10.

```
  4  7  4  2  7  5  1  4  7  5  2  6  5  10  1  4  5  9  3  5  3  8  9
  10  9  3  7  9  2  4  7  7  1  8  9  2  8
BREAK IN 10
OK
```

★★★

How about random numbers from 1 to 100? Simple!

```
10 ? INT(100*RND(1))+1; : GOTO 10
RUN
  65  42  76  57  63  5  57  27  7  22  52  88  9  60  83  42  90  32
  83  98  44  62  11  11  64  80  90  54  31  72  91  45  14  86  85  81
  35  80  90  15  95  71  47  93  74  82  19  96  8  93  83  79  85
BREAK IN 10
OK
```

Go ahead and try it for numbers between 1 and 1000. Feeling sharp? Then
how about random numbers between 1 and 6? Between 50 and 100?

77

Now that you are getting along so well in learning BASIC, try the following program that uses your accumulated knowledge of BASIC for a game that you and your friends can play with the computer. Yes, a real "game-playing" program, fans! Before typing in the program, go through it and try to understand how it works, line by line. If you get confused, see the next page for explanation. Notice that we use REMark statements. They help somebody who is studying a LISTing of a program to understand what the following section of the program does. You'll recall that when the program is RUN, the computer skips past the REMarks. You can skip them, too, when you're typing in the program, that is if you want to save a little work or time or computer memory space.

✳
✳

DO IT ... (when you understand what the program does ...)

```
NEW

OK
5 REM-NUMBER    A GUESSING GAME
10 REM-ADAPTED FROM THE BOOK "WHAT TO DO AFTER YOU HIT RETURN"
200 REM-PRINT THE INSTRUCTIONS FOR THE GAME
210 ? "I WILL THINK OF A WHOLE NUMBER FROM 1 TO 100."
220 ? "TRY TO GUESS MY NUMBER. AFTER EACH GUESS, I WILL"
230 ? "TELL YOU IF YOU HAVE GUESSED MY NUMBER, OR IF YOUR"
240 ? "GUESS IS TOO SMALL OR TOO BIG."
300 REM-COMPUTER "THINKS" UP A NUMBER - CALL IT X
310 X=INT(100*RND(1))+1
320 ? : ? "OK, I HAVE A NUMBER. START GUESSING."
400 REM-PLAYER GUESSES, COMPUTER COMPARES AND DECIDES
410 ? : INPUT "WHAT IS YOUR GUESS"; G
420 IF G=X THEN ? "YOU GOT IT!!! LET'S PLAY AGAIN " : GOTO 310
430 IF G<X THEN ? "TOO SMALL. GUESS AGAIN." : GOTO 410
440 ? "TOO BIG. GUESS AGAIN." : GOTO 410
RUN
I WILL THINK OF A WHOLE NUMBER FROM 1 TO 100.
TRY TO GUESS MY NUMBER. AFTER EACH GUESS, I WILL
TELL YOU IF YOU HAVE GUESSED MY NUMBER, OR IF YOUR
GUESS IS TOO SMALL OR TOO BIG.

OK, I HAVE A NUMBER. START GUESSING.

WHAT IS YOUR GUESS? 50
TOO SMALL. GUESS AGAIN.

WHAT IS YOUR GUESS? 75
TOO BIG. GUESS AGAIN.

WHAT IS YOUR GUESS? 60
TOO BIG. GUESS AGAIN.

WHAT IS YOUR GUESS? 55
TOO BIG. GUESS AGAIN.
```

```
WHAT IS YOUR GUESS? 53
TOO BIG. GUESS AGAIN.

WHAT IS YOUR GUESS? 52
TOO BIG. GUESS AGAIN.

WHAT IS YOUR GUESS? 51
YOU GOT IT!!! LET'S PLAY AGAIN

OK, I HAVE A NUMBER. START GUESSING.

WHAT IS YOUR GUESS?

OK
```

NUMBER

EXPLAINED

Don't forget that (1) you can use ? for PRINT when typing in instructions, and (2) a PRINT with no instruction after it leaves a blank line in the printout.

```
310 X=INT(100*RND(1))+1
```

Line 310 gets a random number between 1 and 100 and assigns it to variable X.

```
420 IF G=X THEN ? "YOU GOT IT!!! LET'S PLAY AGAIN " : GOTO 310
```

Line 420 compares the computer's number (value of X) with the player's Guess (value of G), and if they are the same (condition *true*), the computer tells you "YOU GOT IT!"

```
430 IF G<X THEN ? "TOO SMALL. GUESS AGAIN." : GOTO 410
```

Line 430 prints TOO BIG if the Guess G is bigger than X.

```
440 ? "TOO BIG. GUESS AGAIN." : GOTO 410
```

Line 440 is only executed if the IF conditions in Lines 420 and 430 are *false* and the computer "falls through" to Line 440.

Line 440 prints TOO SMALL, because if the guess is not equal to or bigger than the computer's number X, then it must be smaller. The computer doesn't need an IF statement to decide that!

Do you understand how the program works? Then go ahead and enter it and RUN it. Hope you get it all typed in right the first time you try. If you don't and it doesn't RUN, get a LISTing of the program and look for your error(s).

Extra for experts: Develop a version of this game for two players who alternate their guesses until one of them gets the number.

1. If Line 20 in an operating program was 20 PRINT SQR(X) and you got an FC error in Line 20, what can you assume is the problem?

    _____

2. How will the computer calculate the INT value of these numbers?

    3.97 _____ −3.96 _____ 4.1 _____ −4.1 _____

    .2 _____ −.2 _____

3. Write the statement that will calculate and print 30 different random integers between 1 and 6 (like 30 rolls of a die).

4. Want to 'fix' a program? Turn back to the NUMBER program. Make whatever 'fixes' are necessary to make the program count the number of guesses and when you win, have the message print

    "YOU GOT IT IN _____ GUESSES. LET'S PLAY AGAIN."

    (at which point the wisened programmer will reset the guess counter to 0!)

5. A simple CRAPS game. A popular game among gamblers of the world is CRAPS. A player rolls two 6-sided die first to get his POINT and then again and again to try to match his POINT. If he succeeds (you too ladies) he is a winner. If not, you keep on rolling until either you match the POINT or you get a 7, in which case you CRAP out. Then you start again rolling for a new POINT. One hitch . . . if the POINT roll is 7 or 11, you are a winner! Write a program to play this simple version of CRAPS. Once working, you may wish to add to your program such rules as are used in your locale. When testing your program you may want to use the RND(−3) to get the same rolls over and over to be sure all is well.

6. START — a number guessing game. Here are the rules typed by the computer . You don't have to include them in your program.

    "I will think of a whole number from 1 to 100. Try to guess my number. After you guess my number, I will type one or more stars (*). The closer you are to my number, the more stars I will type. One star (*) means you are far away from my number. Seven stars (*******) means you are very, very close to my number!!"

    Logic: If the guess is more than 64 away, one star; 32—63 away, two stars; 16—31 away, 3 stars; 8—15 away, 4 stars; 4—7 away, 5 stars; 2—3 away, 6 stars; 1 away, seven stars. You will need to use the absolute value function, something new to you but easy. One clue ...

    IF ABS(X − Y) = 10 THEN 100

81

READ

Here is a little program that "counts to 7" and in effect tells you how many loops it makes when the program is RUN.

You should notice the end of Line 20, which introduces a handy new BASIC statement. Now what do you suppose it tells the computer to do?

DO IT

```
EW

OK
5 REM-AUTOMATIC LOOP COUNTER
10 F=1
20 IF F>7 THEN ? "NOW F ="; F : STOP
30 ? "F ="; F
40 F=F+1 : GOTO 20
RUN
F = 1
F = 2
F = 3
F = 4
F = 5
F = 6
F = 7
NOW F = 8

BREAK IN 20
OK
```

This line checks to see if the loop has repeated itself more than 7 times.

The value of F changes by +1 each time through the loop, and thus counts off the number of loops.

READ

Do you understand how the program above works? Then try another kind of automatic loop by doing the programs on the next page. These programs use FOR-NEXT loops. They are called FOR-NEXT loops because they use the FOR and NEXT statements. We will show two ways of writing the same program. The first version uses single statement lines. The second version uses a multiple statement to put the FOR-NEXT loop instructions in one program line.

Introducing FOR-NEXT

```
NEW

OK
5 REM-USING THE FOR-NEXT LOOP CONTROL VARIABLE TO COUNT OFF LOOPS
10 FOR F=1 TO 7         This is a FOR statement.
20 ? "F =" ; F
30 NEXT F               This is a NEXT statement.
40 ? "NOW F =" ; F
RUN
F = 1
F = 2
F = 3
F = 4
F = 5
F = 6
F = 7
NOW F = 8

OK
```

FIRST VERSION

Now do the following program, and compare it to the one you just tried.
Lines 10, 20 and 30 of the first version are all in one multiple statement line,
Line 10 in the second version.

```
NEW

OK
10 FOR F=1 TO 7 : ? "F =" ; F : NEXT F
20 ? "NOW F =" ; F
RUN
F = 1
F = 2
F = 3
F = 4
F = 5
F = 6
F = 7
NOW F = 8

OK
```

SECOND VERSION

the **FOR~NEXT LOOP** explained

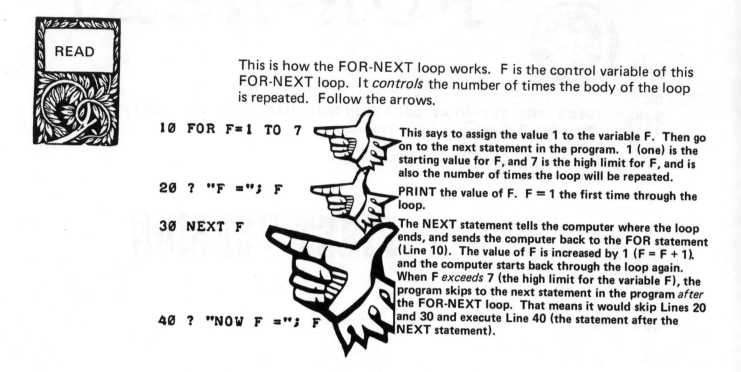

READ

This is how the FOR-NEXT loop works. F is the control variable of this FOR-NEXT loop. It *controls* the number of times the body of the loop is repeated. Follow the arrows.

```
10 FOR F=1 TO 7
```
This says to assign the value 1 to the variable F. Then go on to the next statement in the program. 1 (one) is the starting value for F, and 7 is the high limit for F, and is also the number of times the loop will be repeated.

```
20 ? "F ="; F
```
PRINT the value of F. F = 1 the first time through the loop.

```
30 NEXT F
```
The NEXT statement tells the computer where the loop ends, and sends the computer back to the FOR statement (Line 10). The value of F is increased by 1 (F = F + 1), and the computer starts back through the loop again. When F *exceeds* 7 (the high limit for the variable F), the program skips to the next statement in the program *after* the FOR-NEXT loop. That means it would skip Lines 20 and 30 and execute Line 40 (the statement after the NEXT statement).

```
40 ? "NOW F ="; F
```

Here is the general form for a FOR-NEXT loop.

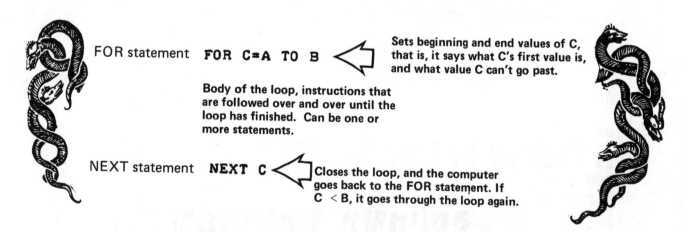

FOR statement   **FOR C=A TO B**   Sets beginning and end values of C, that is, it says what C's first value is, and what value C can't go past.

Body of the loop, instructions that are followed over and over until the loop has finished. Can be one or more statements.

NEXT statement   **NEXT C**   Closes the loop, and the computer goes back to the FOR statement. If C < B, it goes through the loop again.

A FOR statement must always have a NEXT statement matching it to tell the computer where the loop ends, and to send it back to the FOR statement to start the loop again. However, the variable may be omitted after NEXT *if* your program is simple, and *if* leaving out the variable after NEXT doesn't confuse you or the computer.

practice makes purfect

Here are some practice programs using FOR-NEXT loops.

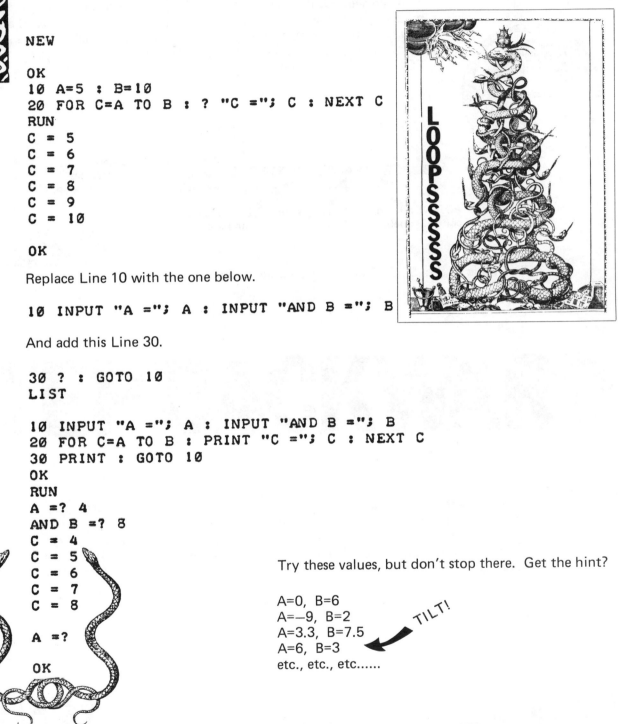

```
NEW

OK
10 A=5 : B=10
20 FOR C=A TO B : ? "C ="; C : NEXT C
RUN
C = 5
C = 6
C = 7
C = 8
C = 9
C = 10

OK
```

Replace Line 10 with the one below.

```
10 INPUT "A ="; A : INPUT "AND B ="; B
```

And add this Line 30.

```
30 ? : GOTO 10
LIST

10 INPUT "A ="; A : INPUT "AND B ="; B
20 FOR C=A TO B : PRINT "C ="; C : NEXT C
30 PRINT : GOTO 10
OK
RUN
A =? 4
AND B =? 8
C = 4
C = 5
C = 6
C = 7
C = 8

A =?

OK
```

Try these values, but don't stop there. Get the hint?

```
A=0,  B=6
A=−9, B=2
A=3.3, B=7.5
A=6,  B=3
etc., etc., etc......
```

TILT!

STEPping Right Along...

You can see that the value of the FOR-NEXT loop control variable automatically increases by 1 each time through the loop. But BASIC also allows you to control the size of the increase in the FOR variable. Here is a new fancier FOR-NEXT loop, with three arguments or parameters for the FOR—NEXT loop control variable.

READ

```
20 FOR C=A TO B STEP S
```

FOR-NEXT loop control variable.

Starting value for C.

Last value C can have.

S is the size of the steps that the C variable increases by each time through the loop.

The value of S in STEP S could be a whole number or a fraction.

STEP BACKWARD

Note that the value of a FOR-NEXT control variable may be *decreased* each time through the loop. This is accomplished by using a negative value for STEP. But it won't run through the loop more than once if the value of A is less than the value of B. The first time the computer comes to NEXT and compares the value of C to the value of B and finds C is less, it ends the loop and goes on to the rest of the program past the FOR-NEXT loop.

FOR more practice do the NEXT page

Try these input values and what ever else you want to try.

A=1, B=10, STEP=2
A=1, B=6, STEP=.7
A=6, B=1, STEP=—1.5
etcetera, etctera, etcetera...

```
NEW

OK
5 REM-FOR STATEMENT WITH STEP
10 INPUT "A ="; A : INPUT "B ="; B : INPUT "STEP"; S
20 FOR C=A TO B STEP S : ? "C ="; C : NEXT C
30 ? "OUT OF THE LOOP BECAUSE C ="; C : GOTO 10
RUN
A =? 1
B =? 10
STEP? 2
C = 1
C = 3
C = 5
C = 7
C = 9
OUT OF THE LOOP BECAUSE C = 11
A =? 1
B =? 6
STEP? .7
C = 1
C = 1.7
C = 2.4
C = 3.1
C = 3.8
C = 4.5
C = 5.2
C = 5.9
OUT OF THE LOOP BECAUSE C = 6.6
A =? 6
B =? 1
STEP? -1.5
C = 6
C = 4.5
C = 3
C = 1.5
OUT OF THE LOOP BECAUSE C = 0
A =?

OK
```

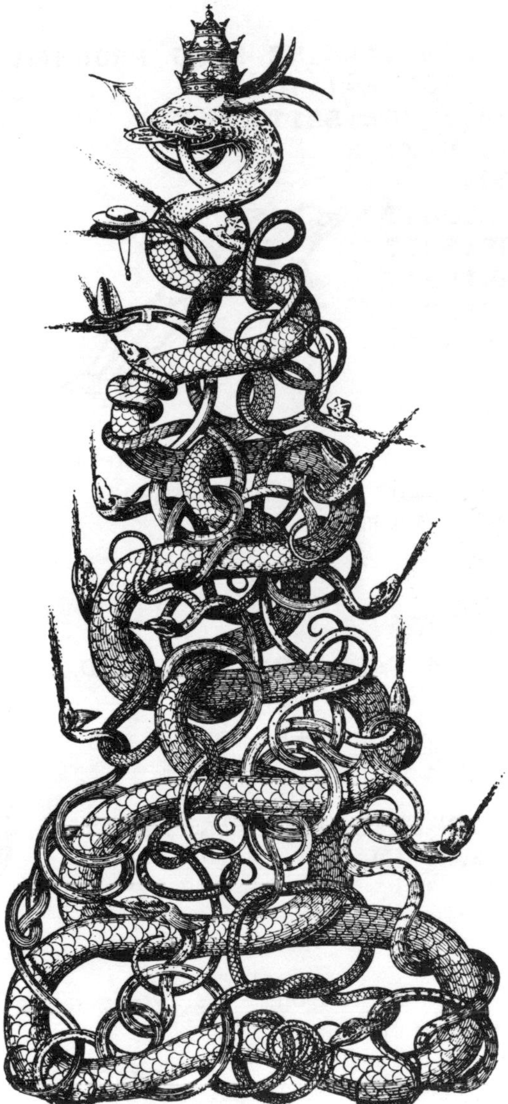

We stopped here (using RETURN to get out of the INPUT loop), BUT
WE SURE HOPE YOU DIDN'T!!!

FROGS?? GIGGLES??? GET SERIOUS!!!

DO IT

Try some other FOR-NEXT loops. Try changing the body of the loop to do something besides tell you the value of C each time through the loop. Experiment!

Try this talking frog program.

```
NEW

OK
5 REM-TALKING FROG PROGRAM
10 FOR K=1 TO 5
20 ? "GRIBBIT"
30 NEXT K
RUN
GRIBBIT
GRIBBIT
GRIBBIT
GRIBBIT
GRIBBIT

OK
```

And now a program that simulates a whole pond full of frogs. (Anyone for frogs legs?)

```
NEW

OK
5 REM-TALKING FROG POND
10 FOR K=1 TO 200
20 ? "GRIBBIT ";
30 NEXT K
RUN
GRIBBIT GRIBBIT GRIBBIT
BREAK IN 20
OK
```

Special note to frog haters: you can use CONTROL/C to stop a FOR-NEXT loop from looping.

88

FOR~NEXT in direct mode

READ

Note that you can put a FOR—NEXT statement and the body or working section that comes between the FOR and NEXT statements, in a one line multiple statement. That means you can use FOR—NEXT in one line *direct mode* instructions. Of course, it only works if all the instructions will fit on one line. Try the ones below.

Tickle your computer's fancy with this direct mode statement to give the computer the giggles.

```
H$="HA " : FOR C=1 TO 50 : ? H$; : NEXT C
HA HA HA HA HA HA HA HA HA HA HA HA HA HA HA HA HA HA HA HA HA HA HA HA
HA HA HA HA HA HA HA HA HA HA HA HA HA HA HA HA HA HA HA HA HA HA HA HA
HA HA
OK
```

Now use direct mode to print a table of squares and square roots for 1 to 16.

This part PRINTs the headings...   ...and this part does the table. Aren't FOR—NEXT loops wonderful?

```
? " X", " X↑2", " SQR(X)" : FOR X=1 TO 16 : ? X, X↑2, SQR(X) : NEXT X
  X                X↑2          SQR(X)
  1                1            1
  2                4            1.41421
  3                9            1.73205
  4                16           2
  5                25           2.23607
  6                36           2.44949
  7                49           2.64575
  8                64           2.82843
  9                81           3
  10               100          3.16228
  11               121          3.31663
  12               144          3.4641
  13               169          3.60555
  14               196          3.74166
  15               225          3.87298
  16               256          4
OK
```

Try your own FOR-NEXT loop ideas. Do it now!

The Last Word

READ

DO IT

The FOR—NEXT loop control variable *parameters* (the beginning and ending values and the size of the STEPs) can be expressions to be computed when the program is RUN. Our demo below shows several possibilities, including the application of functions to get these parameters or values.

```
A=16 : Y=2.185 : FOR X=SQR(A) TO A/2 STEP INT(Y) : ? X : NEXT X
4
6
8

OK
```

All the parameters for the control variable may be expressions requiring calculations. The computer does the calculations the first time it sees the FOR statement in a RUN of the program, just before it starts to execute the body of the FOR-NEXT loop. The FOR arguments do not change, that is, they are *not* recalculated each time the computer goes through the loop during the same RUN.

DO IT

NEW

FOR-NEXT loops are handy for any repeated action. Let's use a FOR-NEXT loop to print a table of information. The body of the loop is a formula for calculating interest on money, such as a savings account in a bank. The formula stays the same, but the values used in the formula can change for each trip through the loop. We use the STEP function to see how our savings gathers interest for different rates of interest (variable 1 in the program below). We want to know how our savings increases if the interest rate is increased by 1/4%, over a range of 5% to 8%.

```
OK
5 REM-SIMPLE INTEREST COMPOUNDED YEARLY, 5 TO 8% IN 1/4% STEPS
10 REM-PRINT HEADINGS AND TABLE OF RETURN ON $500 IN 5 YEARS
100 PRINT "INTEREST", "PRINCIPAL + INTEREST"
110 PRINT "  RATE", "     (FIVE YEARS)"
120 FOR I=5 TO 8 STEP .25
130 R=500*(1+I/100)↑5
140 PRINT I, R
150 NEXT I
OK
RUN
```

INTEREST RATE	PRINCIPAL + INTEREST (FIVE YEARS)
5	638.141
5.25	645.774
5.5	653.479
5.75	661.259
6	669.113
6.25	677.041
6.5	685.044
6.75	693.121
7	701.276
7.25	709.507
7.5	717.815
7.75	726.199
8	734.664

OK

See the neatly spaced heading for the table, using two PRINT statements (Lines 100 and 110).

YOU do it: Use your vast knowledge of BASIC to make the computer round off the PRINTed values to the nearest cent.

loops inside of loops

READ

You can use one FOR ... NEXT loop *inside* another FOR ... NEXT loop. In computer jargon, they say one loop is *nested* inside the other loop. However, you can't "overlap" two loops, that is, with the NEXT statement for the first FOR coming *before* the NEXT statement for the second FOR. It's easy to understand by looking at it.

RIGHT

```
NEW

OK
5 REM-NESTED FOR-NEXT LOOPS
10 FOR A=1 TO 3
20 FOR B=1 TO 5
30 ? "NESTED LOOPS"
40 NEXT B
50 NEXT A
RUN
NESTED LOOPS
NESTED LOOPS
NESTED LOOPS
NESTED LOOPS
NESTED LOOPS
NESTED LOOPS
NESTED LOOPS
NESTED LOOPS
NESTED LOOPS
NESTED LOOPS
NESTED LOOPS
NESTED LOOPS
NESTED LOOPS
NESTED LOOPS
NESTED LOOPS

OK
```

This loop is nested inside this loop

MORAL: Crossed loops are a no—no!

wrong

```
5 REM-CROSSED FOR-NEXT LOOPS
10 FOR A=1 TO 3
20 FOR B=1 TO 5
30 PRINT "CROSSED LOOPS"
40 NEXT A
50 NEXT B
RUN
CROSSED LOOPS
CROSSED LOOPS
CROSSED LOOPS

?NF ERROR IN 50
OK
```

These loops overlap, and therefore are not nested one inside the other.

NF ERROR means Next without For. This means the computer came to a NEXT statement, but since the loops were crossed, it could not find the FOR statement with the same control variable. Notice that the computer did execute the first FOR—NEXT loop with the control variable A. But then the computer just followed the rules for the way FOR—NEXT loops operate. After the third time through the loop, A=4, so the computer went on to the next statement after 40 NEXT A. That means it came to 50 NEXT B directly from the A loop. The computer thought it had found a NEXT statement (NEXT B) without a FOR statement with the same control variable. That's why it said NF ERROR IN 50. Now if a smart person like you is confused, imagine what happens to a dumb machine like the computer.

91

NESTED LOOPS

Here are two more demonstrations of the mechanics of nested FOR—NEXT loops. Look carefully to see which loop is providing the output when you RUN the program. Notice that for each trip through the outside loop, the inside loop goes through its complete cycle of loops.

READ

DO IT

```
NEW

OK
5 REM-NESTED LOOPS REVISITED
10 FOR A=1 TO 3
20 PRINT "NESTED"
30 FOR B=1 TO 4
40 PRINT "          LOOPS"
50 NEXT B
60 NEXT A
RUN
NESTED
          LOOPS
          LOOPS      FOR B=1 TO 4
          LOOPS
          LOOPS
NESTED
          LOOPS
          LOOPS      FOR B=1 TO 4
          LOOPS
          LOOPS
NESTED
          LOOPS
          LOOPS      FOR B=1 TO 4
          LOOPS
          LOOPS

OK
```

FOR A=1 TO 3

```
NEW

OK
5 REM-CONTROL VARIABLE VALUES
10 FOR A=1 TO 3
20 FOR B=1 TO 5
30 PRINT "A ="; A; "B ="; B,
40 NEXT B
50 NEXT A
RUN
```

See here? Look at the first line of output. The value of control variable A stays at 1 until the B loop has gone to its limit (B=1 TO 5). Now look at the second line of output. A has increased by 1, so that now A=2, while B goes to its limit again. And so on for the next line of output.

⇓ ⇓   ⇓ ⇓   ⇓ ⇓   ⇓ ⇓   ⇓ ⇓   ⇓ ⇓

A = 1 B = 1	A = 1 B = 2	A = 1 B = 3	A = 1 B = 4	A = 1 B = 5
A = 2 B = 1	A = 2 B = 2	A = 2 B = 3	A = 2 B = 4	A = 2 B = 5
A = 3 B = 1	A = 3 B = 2	A = 3 B = 3	A = 3 B = 4	A = 3 B = 5

OK

Notice that if you are using more than one FOR-NEXT loop (nested loops in particular) it is wise to specify after NEXT which FOR variable is getting increased by the NEXT statement, such as NEXT A for the first FOR variable A, and NEXT B for the second FOR variable B.

Still feeling adventureous? Try a program with bare NEXT's, that is, without the variable after NEXT.

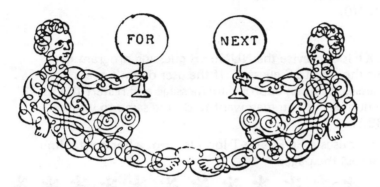

FOR-NEXT

Executes a controlled loop between the FOR and the NEXT statements for a specified number of times.

    line no. FOR (variable) = expression to expression STEP expression
    line no. NEXT (variable)

10 FOR X = 1 TO 30	1 is initial value of X, 30 is final value of X,
20 PRINT X,	no STEP is specified, therefore implied to
30 NEXT X	be one (1). It will print values 1 — 30 and
40 END	then continue to next statement (END).

10 FOR 2 = N TO M	N, M must have been previously defined values.

10 FOR Z = 1 TO 2 STEP .1	Will print value 1 - 2 in increments
20 PRINT Z,	of .1
30 NEXT Z	1.1, 1.2, 1.3, 1.4, 1.5, . . . 2.0

10 FOR X = 30 TO N STEP −1	Will count down (negative increments)
	from 30 to N.

1. What happens in this program?

   ```
   10 FOR X = 17 TO 5
   20 PRINT X,
   30 NEXT X
   ```

2. What is wrong with this program to print a table of 20 different random numbers?

   ```
   10 FOR X = 1 TO 20
   20 PRINT "NO." , "RANDOM NO."
   30  PRINT X, RND(0)
   40  NEXT
   ```

3. Using a FOR-NEXT loop, revise the NUMBER guessing program in Chapter 6 to limit the user to 8 guesses. If the user doesn't guess correctly by 8 guesses, print an appropriate message and restart the game with a new number. (You may want to do the same to your version of STARS.)

4. Write a program that uses a FOR-NEXT loop to print a horizontal line of * all the way across the page.

   *

5. The savings and loan industry is very competitive giving you a choice as to how much interest you can earn and how long you must leave it in to earn that interest. Write a program using NESTED FOR-NEXT loops to print a table as shown below. Assume you have 10,000 to deposit and that interest is compounded once a year (if you know how to compound quarterly or "continuously", please do it!).

YEARS	5%	5.50%	6.00%	6.50%
5				
10				
15				
20				
25				

6. You have 20 employees. Their payroll information is contained in 20 DATA statements as follows: 900 DATA name (N$), hours worked, hourly wage. Write a program to compute the weekly gross pay of each and print the results in a simple report form. You pay your help time and ½ for all hours worked over 40 per week.

95

FUNCTION JUNCTION #2

BASIC provides you with a variety of functions for manipulating strings. In this section we will play with strings, word games you might call it. We will also introduce some other special functions.

LEN( ) String or string variable

LEN(X$) is the function in BASIC that makes the computer tell you how long a string is. (Remember that spaces and punctuation marks are also characters in a string as far as the computer is concerned.)

DO IT

```
NEW

OK
10 INPUT "YOUR NAME";N$
20 ? N$; " HAS"; LEN(N$); "CHARACTERS."
RUN
YOUR NAME? JERALD R. BROWN
JERALD R. BROWN HAS 15 CHARACTERS.

OK


NEW

OK
10 B$="INSTANT BASIC IS EASY" : ? LEN(B$)
RUN
 21
```

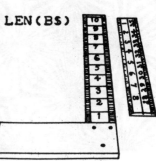

Now, let's put three more functions through some paces, and then we'll explain in full. You can get a first clue as to what parts of a string are manipulated by these functions, just by looking at their names: LEFT$, RIGHT$, and MID$. Note how we use the value of LEN(I$) to establish the limit of the FOR-NEXT loop control variable.

```
NEW

OK
10 IS="INSTANT BASIC"
20 FOR K=1 TO LEN(IS)
30 ? LEFTS(IS,K)
40 NEXT K
RUN
I
IN
INS
INST
INSTA
INSTAN
INSTANT
INSTANT
INSTANT B
INSTANT BA
INSTANT BAS
INSTANT BASI
INSTANT BASIC

OK
```

Note the use of control variable K to specify how many characters are PRINTed by the LEFT$ function.

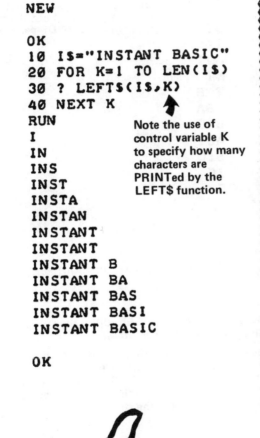

Now replace line 30 and RUN the program again. (LIST if you want to.)

```
30 ? RIGHTS(IS,K)

RUN
C
IC
SIC
ASIC
BASIC
 BASIC
T BASIC
NT BASIC
ANT BASIC
TANT BASIC
STANT BASIC
NSTANT BASIC
INSTANT BASIC

OK
```

LEFT$( )

RIGHT$( )

MID$( )

Yet another string manipulating function, in another line 30.
Again LIST if you want to see the whole program before you RUN it.

DO IT

```
30 ? MIDS(IS,K,1), MIDS(IS,K,3)
RUN
I            INS
N            NST
S            STA
T            TAN
A            ANT
N            NT
T            T B
             BA
B            BAS
A            ASI
S            SIC
I            IC
C            C

OK
```

**Note the two different MID$ functions.
What can you tell about the third
argument in the MID$ parentheses?**

READ

Have you figured out what LEN, LEFT$, RIGHT$ and MID$ instruct the
computer to do?

LEN ( )   gives you the number of characters (LENgth) in the string assigned to
          the string variable you put in the parentheses.

LEFT$ ( ) gives you all the characters in the string identified by the string variable,
          starting with the character number that follows the string variable inside
          the parentheses. For example, LEFT$(X$,4) says to return the part
          of the string assigned to X$, including the 4th character from the *left*
          and all the ones to the *left* of it in the string.

Use direct mode to demonstrate how LEFT$ works. First, assign a string of
numbers to the string variable X$, and have the computer return only the
left 4 characters of the string. Then assign the string "COMPUTERS" to the
string variable Y$ and have the computer return only the left 4 characters
of this string.

DO IT

```
X$="123456789" : ? LEFTS(X$,4)
1234

OK

Y$="COMPUTERS" : ? LEFTS(Y$,4)
COMP

OK
```

L E F T $

98

RIGHT$ ( ) gives you all the characters in the string starting at the character with the position number identified and going on to the right end of the string. RIGHT$(X$,4) says to return the part of the string assigned to X$, starting with the 4th character from the *right end* of the string, *and* all the characters to the *right* of it in the string.

With the strings assigned to X$ and Y$ still in the computer's memory, you can enter direct mode statements to show how RIGHT$ works.

```
? RIGHTS(XS,4)
6789

OK

? RIGHTS(YS,4)
TERS

OK
```

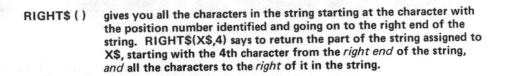

MID$ ( ) returns the part of the string identified by the numbers following the string variable inside the parentheses. The first number says where to start, and the second number tells how many characters to PRINT. If there is no second number in the MID$ argument, the computer starts at the specified character and prints that character and the rest of the string.

Example: MID$(X$, 4) says to return the part of the string starting with the 4th character, and including the rest of the string. MID$(X$, 4, 3) says to return the part of the string starting with the 4th character, but only that character and the next 2 characters (3 characters total are returned).

With the X$ string of numbers and the Y$ string of letters still in the computer's memory, use direct mode to demonstrate the two forms of the MID$ function for both strings.

```
? MIDS(XS,4), MIDS(XS,4,3)
456789         456

OK

? MIDS(YS,4), MIDS(YS,4,3)
PUTERS         PUT

OK
```

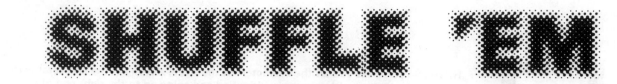

You can reshuffle the characters in a string using these string functions, joining the pieces together with + (plus sign). That's called (are you ready) concatenation. Check your dictionary.

DO IT

Invent your own insult:

```
10 MS="HELLO TODAY, GOODBYE"
20 XS=MIDS(MS,14,2)+MIDS(MS,6,1)+MIDS(MS,7,2)+MIDS(MS,13,1)+LEFTS(MS,4)
30 PRINT XS
OK
RUN
CENSORED


OK
NEW


OK
10 XS="ABCDEFGHIJKLMNOPQRSTUVWXYZ"
20 FOR K=1 TO LEN(XS) : AS=MIDS(XS,K,1) : ? AS; " = "; ASC(AS) : NEXT K
RUN
A =   65
B =   66
C =   67
D =   68
E =   69
F =   70
G =   71
H =   72
I =   73
J =   74
K =   75
L =   76
M =   77
N =   78
O =   79
P =   80
Q =   81
R =   82
S =   83
T =   84
U =   85
V =   86
W =   87
X =   88
Y =   89
Z =   90

OK
```

We used control variable K in the MID$ function to pick out each letter in its turn and assign it to A$.

Every character on the keyboard has a numerical equivalent to the computer, called its ASCII number. Who's ASCII? It's the American Standard Code for Information Interchange. (Just thought you'd like to know.) The ASC function gives the ASCII number for a string character.

KEEPING SECRETS

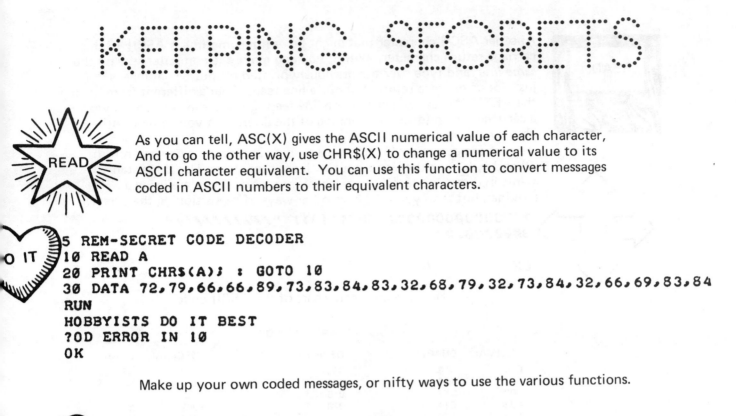

As you can tell, ASC(X) gives the ASCII numerical value of each character, And to go the other way, use CHR$(X) to change a numerical value to its ASCII character equivalent. You can use this function to convert messages coded in ASCII numbers to their equivalent characters.

```
5 REM-SECRET CODE DECODER
10 READ A
20 PRINT CHR$(A); : GOTO 10
30 DATA 72,79,66,66,89,73,83,84,83,32,68,79,32,73,84,32,66,69,83,84
RUN
HOBBYISTS DO IT BEST
?OD ERROR IN 10
OK
```

Make up your own coded messages, or nifty ways to use the various functions.

"One Ringee Dingee..."

Are your ears ringing? How about your terminal? There is a character called BEL, recognized by BASIC as ASCII number 7. If you use this character in a PRINT statement, it will cause a bell to ring on most terminals, or a "beep" on many CRT's. BEL is a favorite with computer game programmers to signal a correct answer, an error, or just to keep up interest. To ring the BEL, try the following two instructions in direct mode.

```
? CHR$(7)

OK
```

◁ No visual output, just a ringing in your ear.

```
FOR J=1 TO 8 : ? CHR$(7) : NEXT J
```

◀ Eight bells and all is well. Also eight line spaces, one for each time the ? (PRINT) statement is performed.

```
OK
```

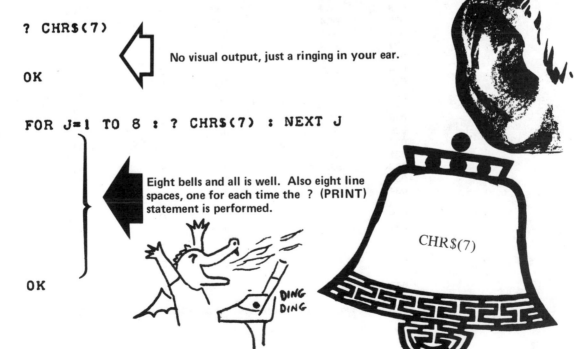

CHR$(7)

101

READ

Another ASCII character that might be useful sometime is ASCII 13, the carriage return character. With it you can make the computer stay on the *same line*, and type over the previously printed output. That means it just does a carriage return, but *not* a line feed. That's different from hitting the RETURN key, which causes a line feed (goes to the next line down)*and* a carriage return (goes to beginning of the line). Can you think of other uses for this character?

Instruct the computer (1) to type a string, (2) then do a carriage return, (3) and type over the last output with another string. Use three statements in direct mode. (Note: this may not work if you are using a CRT terminal, but then you may have other ways of repositioning the cursor.)

DO IT

```
? "0000000000"; CHR$(13); "//////////"
0000000000
```

OK

Here is a complete chart of the ASCII code.

ASCII CHARACTER CODES

DECIMAL	CHAR.	DECIMAL	CHAR.	DECIMAL	CHAR.
000	NUL	043	+	086	V
001	SO11	044	,	087	W
002	STX	045	–	088	X
003	ETX	046	.	089	Y
004	EOT	047	/	090	Z
005	ENQ	048	0	091	[
006	ACK	049	1	092	\
007	BEL	050	2	093	]
008	BS	051	3	094	↑
009	HT	052	4	095	←
010	LF	053	5	096	`
011	VT	054	6	097	a
012	FF	055	7	098	b
013	CR	056	8	099	c
014	SO	057	9	100	d
015	SI	058	:	101	e
016	DLE	059	;	102	f
017	DCI	060	<	103	g
018	DC2	061	=	104	h
019	DC3	062	>	105	i
020	DC4	063	?	106	j
021	NAK	064	@	107	k
022	SYN	065	A	108	l
023	ETB	066	B	109	m
024	CAN	067	C	110	n
025	EM	068	D	111	o
026	SUB	069	E	112	p
027	ESCAPE	070	F	113	q
028	FS	071	G	114	r
029	GS	072	H	115	s
030	RS	073	I	116	t
031	US	074	J	117	u
032	SPACE	075	K	118	v
033	!	076	L	119	w
034	"	077	M	120	x
035	#	078	N	121	y
036	$	079	O	122	z
037	%	080	P	123	{
038	&	081	Q	124	¦
039	'	082	R	125	}
040	(	083	S	126	~
041	)	084	T	127	DEL
042	*	085	U		

LF=Line Feed   FF=Form Feed   CR=Carriage Return   DEL=Rubout

Taking Care of Business

CREAD String information stored in DATA statements in a standardized form can be manipulated with the string functions you have learned. Here is a simple example. Let's say your computer club has five members, and you have decided to "computerize" your mailing list of members. Here is the form in which your DATA is entered, with the information for each member entered in a separate DATA statement. The name and address of each member is entered as one data item (no commas) per DATA statement.

J.R. BROWN	321 MILLBAY ST.	SAN FRANCISCO	CA94123
TIM KELLEY	48 S. AVALON	IOWA CITY	IA52240
M.J. MCPHEE	1010 DOYLE	MENLO PARK	CA94025
LEROY FINKEL	888 CONSTANCE	MENLO PARK	CA94025
M. SPILANE	98354 SKYLINE	LA HONDA	CA95040

You may find it helpful to fill in the form, and then type in the DATA. That way it is easy to count the spaces that must be left between the parts of each data item.

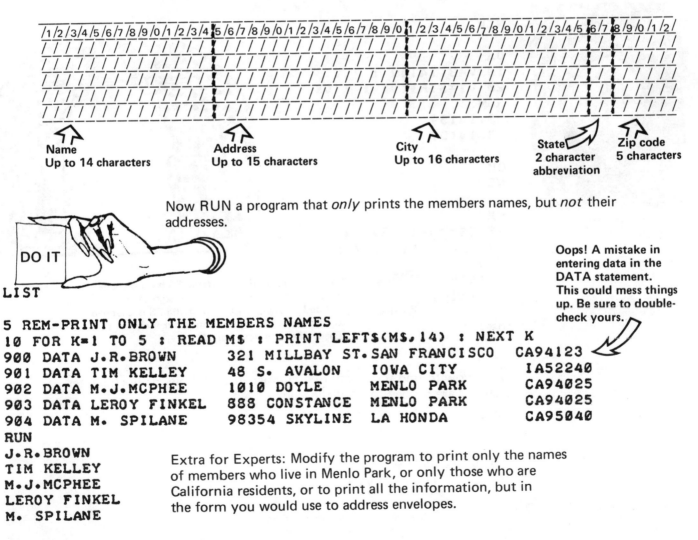

Name Up to 14 characters

Address Up to 15 characters

City Up to 16 characters

State 2 character abbreviation

Zip code 5 characters

Now RUN a program that *only* prints the members names, but *not* their addresses.

DO IT

LIST

Oops! A mistake in entering data in the DATA statement. This could mess things up. Be sure to double-check yours.

```
5 REM-PRINT ONLY THE MEMBERS NAMES
10 FOR K=1 TO 5 : READ M$ : PRINT LEFT$(M$,14) : NEXT K
900 DATA J.R.BROWN        321 MILLBAY ST.SAN FRANCISCO    CA94123
901 DATA TIM KELLEY       48 S. AVALON   IOWA CITY        IA52240
902 DATA M.J.MCPHEE       1010 DOYLE     MENLO PARK       CA94025
903 DATA LEROY FINKEL     888 CONSTANCE  MENLO PARK       CA94025
904 DATA M. SPILANE       98354 SKYLINE  LA HONDA         CA95040
RUN
J.R.BROWN
TIM KELLEY
M.J.MCPHEE
LEROY FINKEL
M. SPILANE
```

Extra for Experts: Modify the program to print only the names of members who live in Menlo Park, or only those who are California residents, or to print all the information, but in the form you would use to address envelopes.

OK

presto change-o!

It is possible to convert a number to a string, or a string to a number. The function that converts a number to a string is STR$(X). Changing a number to a string means that the string representation cannot be used in calculations, but you can use all the other string functions to manipulate the number turned string.

To change the string representation to a number, use the VAL(X$) function.

STR$(X)

⇧
The value to be changed
to a string goes here.

VAL(X$)

⇧
The string to be changed
to a numerical value goes
here.

```
NEW

OK
10 V=3.14159 : ? V
20 V$=STR$(V) : ? V$
RUN
 3.14159
 3.14159

OK
NEW

OK
10 S$="3.14159" : ? S$
20 S=VAL(S$) : ? S
RUN
3.14159
 3.14159

OK
```

Notice something? The string S$ has no space in front of the number for a — sign or the assumed + sign. When the string S$ is changed to a value, however, the computer includes that space. (See the next page.)

Here's how to find the length of a number, that is, how many character positions are needed to print the value.

```
NEW

OK
10 V=3.14159
20 ? LEN(STR$(V))
RUN
 8

OK
```

Is the computer right?
Go on to the next page. ➤

First change V to a string, then
find the LENgth of the string.

104

NOSPACE

READ

Remember that BASIC leaves one character space in front of a positive value for the + sign even though it doesn't print it. When a positive value is changed to a string with STR$, the string also includes that space. Count the characters in the output from the last program to verify this. Remember that the decimal point is also counted as a character.

Converting a value to a string gives you more control over how and where that number is printed by the computer. This is because you can apply string functions to a "converted" value.

Let's say we want to print the value of a FOR-NEXT variable one after another.

DO IT

```
NEW
OK
10 FOR K=1 TO 8 : PRINT K; : NEXT K : PRINT
20 FOR K=1 TO 8 : K$=STR$(K) : PRINT MID$(K$,2); : NEXT K
RUN
 1  2  3  4  5  6  7  8
12345678
OK
```

We don't want those spaces in there.
So we change the value to a string, and
print the string starting with the second
character. That leaves out the space!

Coming soon — real applications for values converted to strings. Keep an eye out for STR$ used to change values to strings in order to control the print position of numbers.

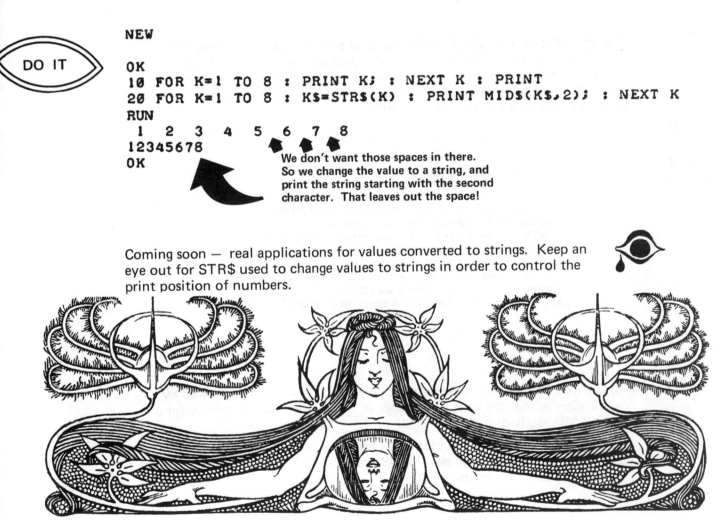

Now let's master another interesting and useful BASIC function that gives you more ways to get what you want out of your computer. The more control you have, the better your programs will be. Each new BASIC function you learn will bring you closer to using BASIC and your computer to the fullest extent possible.

TAB( ), the low calorie function!

If you'll cast your mind back, you'll recall that early in this book we told you about the 72 character positions on a line for most computer terminals. You'll also recall that we said the character positions are numbered from 0 to 71, like this: (read the numbers up and down, $\frac{1}{0}$ = 10 $\frac{7}{1}$ = 71):

```
0123456789111111111122222222223333333333444444444455555555556666666666 77
          0123456789012345678901234567890123456789012345678901234567890 1
```

You can tell the computer at what character position you want something PRINTed by using the TAB(X) function. On a regular typewriter, you can usually set tab positions for typing at various places in a line. The TAB function in BASIC is similar, and is used in PRINT statements to let you control where on a line something is PRINTed.

TAB(X)

The character position (0 to 71) goes here, and tells the computer at what character position it should start PRINTing the next output. The argument can be a number, a variable, or an expression to calculate, but TAB must end up having a positive number between 0 and 71 for its argument. If the argument is a number with a fraction, the TAB function only uses the *whole number* part. For example, TAB(15.7) is executed as TAB(15).

In a PRINT statement (where you usually use it), TAB(X) is followed by a semicolon so that the next output indeed begins at the character position that TAB specified.

And one last note: TAB cannot space the teletypewriter to the left. So, if it is already at character position 45, you cannot TAB back to position 30 or any position before 45.

106

TAB( ), THE ARTIST

In the following program we use the PRINT statement to draw a picture or graphic representation of the Leaning Tower of Pizza (no anchovies, please).

DO IT

```
NEW

OK
10 ? "XXX"
20 ? " XXX"
30 ? "  XXX"
40 ? "   XXX"
50 ? "    XXX"
RUN
XXX
  XXX
    XXX
      XXX
        XXX

OK
```

Now do it with TAB.

```
NEW

OK
10 PRINT TAB(0); "XXX"
20 PRINT TAB(1); "XXX"
30 PRINT TAB(2); "XXX"
40 PRINT TAB(3); "XXX"
50 PRINT TAB(4); "XXX"
OK
RUN
XXX
 XXX
  XXX
   XXX
    XXX

OK
```

How about a more automated tower graphic? Note the use of the FOR-NEXT loop control variable to get the "lean."

```
NEW

OK
10 FOR X=0 TO 4
20 ? TAB(X); "XXX"
30 NEXT X
RUN
XXX
 XXX
  XXX
   XXX
    XXX

OK
```

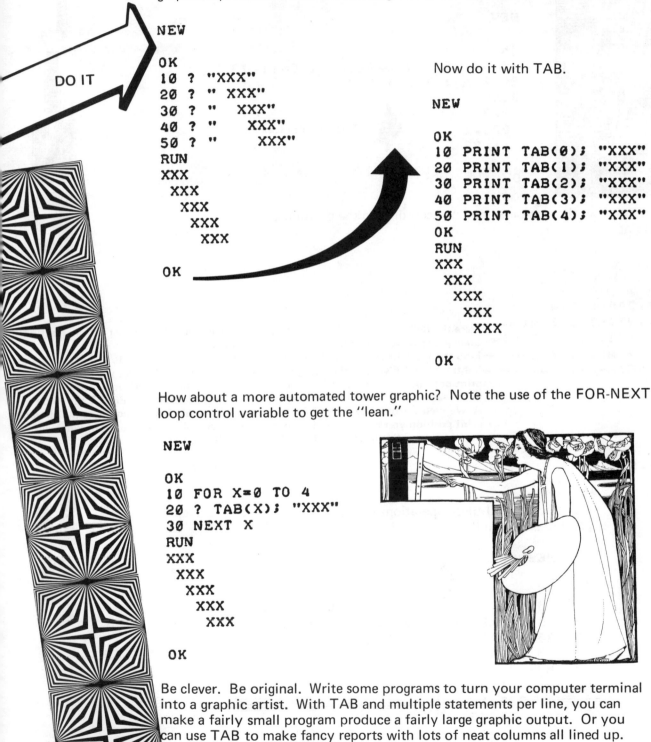

Be clever. Be original. Write some programs to turn your computer terminal into a graphic artist. With TAB and multiple statements per line, you can make a fairly small program produce a fairly large graphic output. Or you can use TAB to make fancy reports with lots of neat columns all lined up.

Now here is another use for TAB in combination with some other functions you have learned.

Let's say you wish to line up a series of numbers according to where the decimal point is located.

First, the numbers are printed as usual.

```
NEW

OK
10 A=1.346 : B=225.1 : C=11.73
20 ? A : ? B : ? C
RUN
 1.346
 225.1
 11.73

OK
```

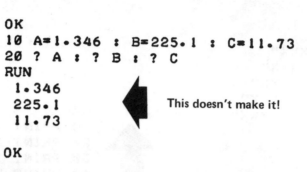
This doesn't make it!

Here is a way to get the numbers lined up according to the position of the decimal point.

```
NEW

OK
10 A=1.346 : ? A
20 A1=INT(A) : ? A1 ◄─── Take the INTeger part of A (that's A up to the decimal point, leaving off the fraction).
30 A$=STR$(A1) : ? A$ ◄─── Change the value to a string with the STR$ function.
40 L=LEN(A$) : ? L ◄─── Find the LENgth of the string—that's the number of characters up to the decimal point.
50 ? TAB(6-L); A ◄─── Subtract the  LENgth of the string from some number, say 6, to get the proper
RUN                    print position to begin PRINTing the number, so that the decimal point always ends up
 1.346                 in the same place. Then TAB to that character print position, and PRINT the value of
 1                     A. We used 6 arbitrarily in the TAB function. You would have to count to the character
 1                     print position you would need for your table, chart, column of figures, or whatever you
 2                     might be using this instruction for.  EXPERIMENT!!!
     1.346

OK
```

Now combine all these operations into one, and remember to keep your parentheses paired!

```
NEW

OK
10 A=1.346 : B=225.1 : C= 11.73
20 ? TAB(6-LEN(STR$(INT(A)))); A
30 ? TAB(6-LEN(STR$(INT(B)))); B
40 ? TAB(6-LEN(STR$(INT(C)))); C
RUN
     1.346
   225.1         ◄─ It's all right now, baby, it's all right now.
    11.73

OK
```

108

For complex drawings, it would be handy to have an easy way to count the TAB location or character position for various parts of the graphic. So we designed a program to make computer drawings easier to program. For a terminal that prints on paper, you can use the program to print a numbered guide to use for your computer drawings. "Connect the dots" and then use the guide to turn your drawing into a computer program that does the drawing. For a CRT, you might try filling the screen with 0's and using a soft grease pencil or *washable* crayon or felt point pen to draw your design. You may wish to use plastic wrap or some other transparent protective cover over the video display screen.

Our program may look complicated at first glance, but if you take it one line at a time and see what part of the output each line corresponds to, the complicated becomes easy. Our variables may also give you a clue.

Line 10 produces the first numbers 0 to 9 in the first line of output. That program line should look familiar: seen it before recently?

Line 20—C1 controls the character print position for the rest of the first line of output. Take the line apart mentally to see how it works. Note how the INT function is used to get ten 1's, then ten 2's, etc.

Line 30 gives us blanks at the first part of the second line of output.

Lines 40, 50, 60—C2 counts the remaining character positions in the second line of output, while the FOR-NEXT loop keeps printing 0 to 9 until C2 = 62. Then the computer branches out of the loop.

Line 70 contains nested FOR-NEXT loops: L counts the number of lines to be printed, and C3 counts off the character print positions in each line.

```
5 REM-PRINT NUMBERED GRID
10 FOR X=0 TO 9 : X$=STR$(X) : PRINT MID$(X$,2); : NEXT X
20 FOR C1=10 TO 71 : C1$=STR$(INT(C1/10)) : PRINT MID$(C1$,2); : NEXT C1
30 FOR Y=0 TO 9 : PRINT " "; : NEXT Y
40 FOR Z=0 TO 9 : Z$=STR$(Z) : PRINT MID$(Z$,2);
50 C2=C2+1 : IF C2=62 THEN 70
60 NEXT Z : GOTO 40
70 FOR L=1 TO 20 : FOR C3=0 TO 71: PRINT "O"; : NEXT C3,L
RUN
0123456789111111111122222222223333333333444444444455555555556666666666677
          012345678901234567890123456789012345678901234567890123456789012345678901
0000000000000000000000000000000000000000000000000000000000000000000000000
0000000000000000000000000000000000000000000000000000000000000000000000000
0000000000000000000000000000000000000000000000000000000000000000000000000
0000000000000000000000000000000000000000000000000000000000000000000000000
0000000000000000000000000000000000000000000000000000000000000000000000000
0000000000000000000000000000000000000000000000000000000000000000000000000
0000000000000000000000000000000000000000000000000000000000000000000000000
0000000000000000000000000000000000000000000000000000000000000000000000000
0000000000000000000000000000000000000000000000000000000000000000000000000
0000000000000000000000000000000000000000000000000000000000000000000000000
0000000000000000000000000000000000000000000000000000000000000000000000000
0000000000000000000000000000000000000000000000000000000000000000000000000
0000000000000000000000000000000000000000000000000000000000000000000000000
0000000000000000000000000000000000000000000000000000000000000000000000000
0000000000000000000000000000000000000000000000000000000000000000000000000
0000000000000000000000000000000000000000000000000000000000000000000000000
0000000000000000000000000000000000000000000000000000000000000000000000000
0000000000000000000000000000000000000000000000000000000000000000000000000
0000000000000000000000000000000000000000000000000000000000000000000000000
OK        Now let your artistic ability combine with your programming skills to make drawings or abstract art.
```

Teach Your Children Well...

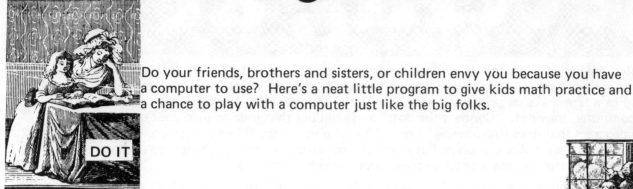

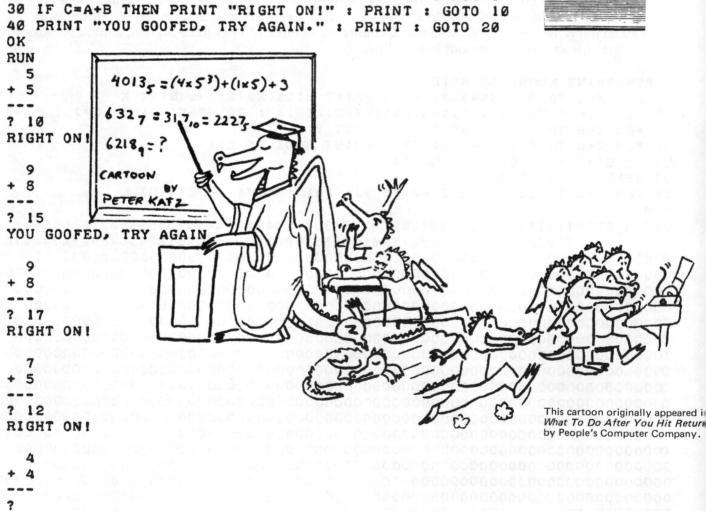

Do your friends, brothers and sisters, or children envy you because you have a computer to use? Here's a neat little program to give kids math practice and a chance to play with a computer just like the big folks.

```
NEW

OK

10 A=INT(RND(1)*10) : B=INT(RND(1)*10)
20 PRINT " ";A : PRINT "+";B : PRINT"---" : INPUT C
30 IF C=A+B THEN PRINT "RIGHT ON!" : PRINT : GOTO 10
40 PRINT "YOU GOOFED, TRY AGAIN." : PRINT : GOTO 20
OK
RUN
    5
+ 5
---
? 10
RIGHT ON!

    9
+ 8
---
? 15
YOU GOOFED, TRY AGAIN

    9
+ 8
---
? 17
RIGHT ON!

    7
+ 5
---
? 12
RIGHT ON!

    4
+ 4
---
?
OK
```

$$4013_5 = (4 \times 5^3) + (1 \times 5) + 3$$

$$632_7 = 31 \cdot 7_{10} = 2227_5$$

$$6218_9 = ?$$

CARTOON BY PETER KAFZ

This cartoon originally appeared in *What To Do After You Hit Return* by People's Computer Company.

Now modify (rewrite and reenter) Line 10 so that the program gives practice with the addition of numbers between 0 and 99.

Change Line 20 so that four dashes or underlines are printed under the numbers in the addition problem.

```
NEW

OK
10 A=INT(RND(1)*100) : B=INT(RND(1)*100)
20 PRINT " "; A : PRINT "+"; B : PRINT "----" : INPUT C
30 IF C=A+B THEN PRINT "RIGHT ON!" : PRINT : GOTO 10
40 PRINT "YOU GOOFED, TRY AGAIN." : PRINT : GOTO 20
OK
RUN
    62
+ 66
----
? 128
RIGHT ON!

    13
+ 84
----
? 97
RIGHT ON!

    77
+ 82
----
? 159
RIGHT ON!

    10
+  4
----
?

OK
```

But look here. This isn't the way you see problems set up in math books.

```
     WRONG              RIGHT

       10                 10
     +  4               +  4
     ----               ----
```

There are as many ways of solving a programming problem as there are of skinning cats. (My apologies to cat lovers.) We could use the TAB function to correctly place the numbers in the problems in standard form, with the 1's in the 1's place and the 10's in the 10's place, and so on for problems with more than two digits.

111

```
NEW

OK
5 REM-NEW IMPROVED ADDITION PRACTICE PROGRAM
10 A=INT(RND(1)*100) : B=INT(RND(1)*100)
20 A$=STR$(A) : B$=STR$(B)
30 ? TAB(5-LEN(A$)); MID$(A$,2) : ? "+"; TAB(5-LEN(B$)); MID$(B$,2)
40 ? "----" : INPUT C
50 IF C=A+B THEN ? "RIGHT ON!!!" : ? : GOTO 10
60 ? "YOU GOOFED, TRY AGAIN." : ? : GOTO 30
RUN
    78
+ 80
----
? 158
RIGHT ON!!!

    54
+ 18
----
? 72
RIGHT ON!!!

    10
+  4
----
? 14
RIGHT ON!!!

     5
+ 30
----
? 35
RIGHT ON!!!

    47
+ 72
----
? 110
YOU GOOFED, TRY AGAIN.
```

Drawing by Marie Marcks reprinted courtesy of Kaiser News ® 1967

READ

EXTRA FOR EXPERTS. (1) You could put a FOR-NEXT loop around the program to give a specified number of problems for one session. (2) You could add a counting statement to Lines 80 and 90 to keep track of right and wrong answers, and to PRINT them at the end of a session. (3) You could limit the number of wrong answers before having the computer give a new problem, by using another FOR-NEXT loop around the central part of the program. (4) You could add PRINT statements to explain how the program is to be used or perhaps, whether to work out the problems on scratch paper before entering the answer, if the problems are complex. (5) You could allow the child to select how many numbers fro each sort of problem. Keep thinking, and happy programming!

FUNCTIONS UNLIMITED: DEFINE YOUR OWN

You can create your own specialized functions, using the DEF FN (Define Function). This is the form in which you DEFine your FuNction for the computer.

READ

DEFine FuNction

DEF FNA (X) = expression in which X is the "dummy variable"

variable argument of the defined function

variable to distinguish this defined function
from any others in the same program

Once you define a function in a program statement, you may use the function just as you would any other function that is part of BASIC. However, there are several tricky things about about defined functions.

(1) You must define your function in the program before you use the function in other statements later on in the program.

(2) DEF is only used in the statement where you DEFine the function.

(3) The "dummy variable" in the DEFinition is just a place holder: it shows the computer where in the function calculations the variable you actually use in the function argument (inside the parentheses) should substitute for the dummy.

(4) Don't be confused: the variable that identifies the function goes right after FN_ where we have the blank. The function argument is the dummy variable (we use V) in the DEF FN_(V) statement, or the real variable when you use the function in a statement.

(5) DEF FN_ may not be used for strings or string variables.

To demonstrate, let's go back to the program we used to line up decimal points. We want a defined function that will provide a value for the TAB argument. We use P (for Point) as the function ID variable.

Every time the computer finds FNP, it does this operation, using the argument variable's value in place of the dummy variable V. The result is a value for the TAB argument.

```
10 A=1.346 : B=225.1 : C= 11.73
20 DEF FNP(V)=6-LEN(STRS(INT(V)))
30 ? TAB(FNP(A)); A
40 ? TAB(FNP(B)); B
50 ? TAB(FNP(C)); C
RUN
      1.346
    225.1
     11.73
```

Sure saved a lot
of typing!

OK

20 DEF FNP(V)=6—LEN(STR$(INT(V)))

dummy variable
function ID (identifying) variable

30 ? TAB(FNP(A)); A

function ID variable

the real variable,
where the dummy variable was.

If you understand the concept of "defining your own" write a program using a DEF FN of use to you for your own interests.

Trigonometery Functions

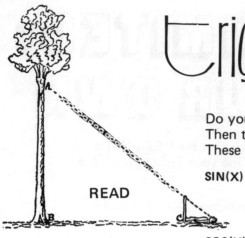

Do your interests (voluntary or otherwise) include the use of trigonometry? Then the following four BASIC functions could be of great help to you. These four functions are:

SIN(X) Gives the sine of the expression X. X is interpreted as being in radians. Note: COS(X) = SIN(X + 3.14159/2) and that 1 Radian = 180/PI degrees which is equal to 57.2958 degrees; so that the sine of X degrees is equal to SIN(X/57.2958).

COS(X) Gives the cosine of the expression X. X is interpreted as being in radians.

TAN(X) Gives the tangent of the expression X. X is interpreted as being in radians.

ATN(X) Gives the arctangent of the argument X. The result is returned in radians and ranges from −PI/2 to PI/2. (PI/2 = 1.5708).

If trigonometry isn't your bag, just note the existence of these functions for future reference, and concentrate instead on the use of BASIC to print (plot) points for a graph.

Plotting Points on a Graph

Our next clever little program demonstrates the use of the computer to plot graphs. We use the SIN(X) function in an expression that provides a TAB value for printing (or *plotting*, to use the mathematicians term) points on a sine wave curve or graph.

The usual method for displaying a sine wave puts the X-axis on the horizontal, and the Y-axis on the vertical like this:

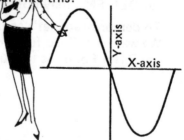

However, most computer terminals cannot backspace, and if the computer is calculating points in sequence along the curve, it becomes a problem. The solution is to print the curve "sideways" like this:

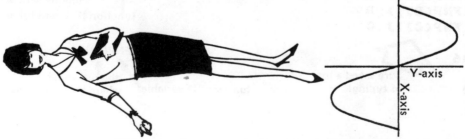

This way the computer can start at the "top" and print points on the curve in succession down the paper or CRT screen.

For any graph, you must decide on a scale that will be both printable by the computer and also show the characteristics of the mathematical function being graphed. Since the sine of an angle can only have values between +1 and −1, we must expand the scale in order to plot a curve that looks like a curve.

TAB(10*(1 + SIN(P)))

Multiplying by 10 gives us an expanded scale of 0 to 20 on the Y-axis, that is, 10 character spaces "above" and "below" the real X-axis. That also means there are 20 character print positions where a point may be plotted or printed by the computer.

Adding one to the value of the sine gives values between 0 and +2, instead of between −1 and +1. The reason for doing this is to avoid negative arguments in the TAB function, since the computer can't TAB to a negative character position. For us non-math types it's sort of like adding a +1 to get a RND number between 1 and 10 instead of 0 and 9 in the RND integer routine we used before.

DO IT

FOR P=0 TO 2*3.14159 STEP .3

By changing this value, we can specify how many cycles will be plotted. 2*PI is one complete cycle, so 4*PI would be 2 cycles.

We can specify how many points we wish plotted along the curve by varying the STEP value. The larger the STEP value, the fewer the points that are plotted.

```
5 REM-PLOTTING A SINE WAVE
10 FOR P=0 TO 2*3.14159 STEP .3
20 PRINT TAB(20*(1+SIN(P)));"X"
30 NEXT P
OK
RUN
```

First Version

Modify the program to see
(1) the effect of changing the number of points plotted;
(2) the effect of changing the "scale expansion factor," and
(3) the effect of changing the number of cycles graphed.

OK

```
10 FOR P=0 TO 4*3.14159 STEP .5
RUN
```
What did we change to get this output?

Second Version

OK

Here's a quicky intro to two more functions. SGN( ) stands for SiGN, and gives you a plus 1 (+1) or a minus one (−1), depending on whether the value in the parentheses is positive or negative. ABS( ) stands for ABSolute value, and gives you the value inside the paraentheses as a positive number, no matter whether the original value was positive *or* negative! We will use these functions here with INT to make the computer always "chop off" the decimal fraction of a value the *same way* no matter whether the value being "chopped" is positive or negative.

SGN(B) can have a value of +1 or −1 only. If the value of B is positive then SGN(B) = +1. If the value of B is negative then SGN(B) = −1. The SGN function gives the computer a way of "remembering" the sign of a value while it performs other operations on the value. Or it may help make a decision in the program, based on whether the value of B is positive or negative.

ABS(B) gives the absolute value of a number. ABS(B) = the positive value of B, whether it was negative or positive to start with.

To *chop* a negative, zero, or positive number, B:

$$A = SGN(B)*INT(ABS(B))$$

Suppose B = −3.1416

$$A = SGN(-3.1416)*INT(ABS(-3.1416))$$
$$= -1*INT(3.1416)$$
$$= -1*3$$
$$= -3$$

CHAPTER 8 PROBLEMS

1. Remember the round off method developed in Chapter 6? It can and should be used in a DEFine function. Write a DEFined function statement that uses this round off method.

2. What will this program print?

   ```
   10 A$ = "BASIC BEST IS INSTANT DOES"
   20 PRINT LEFT(A$,5),
   30 PRINT MID(A$,12,2),
   40 PRINT MID(A$,7,4)
   ```

3. Write a program to print this title backwards: INSTANT BASIC.

4. Assume that you have 20 DATA statements with names of job applicants entered last name first, comma, first name. You want to print a list of these applicants first name first followed by last name. Write a program that will prepare this list. You should use LEN, and MID among other functions.

   DATA ZENITH, HAROLD
   report
   HAROLD ZENITH

5. Modify the addition practice program in this chapter to give the user the choice to add, subtract, multiply, or divide. And for experts, combine all this with the EXTRA FOR EXPERTS tips found in the chapter.

6. What's in a name? A child is born. The family wishes an unusual name, one that starts with the letter J in honor of a deceased grandfather and that is short with no more than 6 letters. Write a program that will generate random names that begin with J. You will have to experiment and come up with some "rules" for how many vowels to use and where they should be placed, otherwise your words will be gibberish ... though unique!

THE REALM OF
SUBSCRIPTED VARIABLES

Now we open up for you the last really important capability of BASIC, one that makes complicated, tedious manipulation of information much easier. This is the realm of *subscripted variables.* Subscripted variables are used to keep track of information in lists and arrays. (Not that you have a complete knowledge of BASIC, mind you, but the other nice little things BASIC can do are like tinsle on the tree.)

This section on subscripted variables will provide you with an important programming tool for an immense variety of programming needs. So pay close attention and don't be afraid to go beyond our examples and **experiment** so that you will feel totally comfortable in dealing with subscripted variables.

You math types may remember subscripts as those little numbers (or letters) at the lower edge of variables in complicated formulas like this:

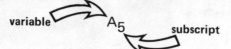

variable A_5 **subscript**

In BASIC, a subscripted variable looks like this:

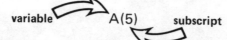

variable $A(5)$ **subscript**

A subscripted string variable could look like this:

string variable $A\$(5)$ **subscript**

The rules about the *variable* part of a subscripted variable are the same as for regular variables and string variables (see page 00 for limitations on variable names.)

Note that $X(3)$ is a subscripted variable. However, note that X, X3, $X(3)$, and $X\$(3)$ are all different variables. They can all be used in the same program, and while they might confuse you, BASIC recognizes them as separate and distinct, and has separate "boxes" for the variables and their values or strings.

Just like a regular variable, a *subscripted variable* names a location inside the computer. We can still think of the locations as those little boxes. Here's what they might look like for subscripted variables.

A(1)

A(0)	2
A(1)	85
A(2)	3
A(3)	6
A(4)	18
A(5)	−55
A(6)	3.98

A set of subscripted variables like this is called an *array*. In particular, this is a *one dimensional array*, also called a *list* or *vector*. The value of A(0) = 2. The value of A(1) = 85. The value of A(4) = A(2)*A(3) or 3*6. Look in the boxes to see the *values* of A(2) and A(3).

118

And Then There's
VARIABLE SUBSCRIPTS

One thing that makes these subscripted variables so handy is that they make it easy to assign a lot of values to a lot of variables. And the reason why they make things easy? Because the subscript for a subscripted variables can also be a variable. (Don't panic, check below.)

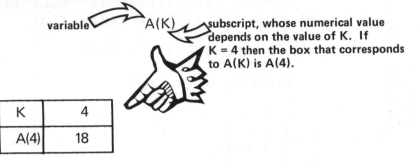

variable → A(K) ← subscript, whose numerical value depends on the value of K. If K = 4 then the box that corresponds to A(K) is A(4).

K	4
A(4)	18

Right off let's be sure we understand that the value of the *subscript* is *not* the value assigned to the *subscripted variable*. This sometimes confuses people at first, so we will make that point several times. In the example above, the value of the *subscript* is 4, and the value of the *subscripted variable* A(4) is 18. Check the boxes.

Don't be afraid to go back and read this introduction over again. When you think you've got the theory down, go on and try out the demonstration programs using subscripted variables.

This program assigns values to four subscripted variables from a DATA statement, then PRINTs the subscripted variables and their assigned values.

```
NEW

OK
5 REM-FIRST SUBSCRIPTED VARIABLE DEMO
10 READ Y(0), Y(1), Y(2), Y(3)
20 ? "Y(0) ="; Y(0)
30 ? "Y(1) ="; Y(1)
40 ? "Y(2) ="; Y(2)
50 ? "Y(3) ="; Y(3)
60 DATA 3, 8, 2, 6.5
RUN
Y(0) = 3
Y(1) = 8
Y(2) = 2
Y(3) = 6.5

OK
```

READ

Now use a FOR-NEXT loop to PRINT the values of the subscripted variables. Notice the use of the FOR-NEXT loop control variable A. For each trip through the loop, the value of A is used to print the subscript of the subscripted variable. It is also used to tell the computer which subcripted variable's assigned *value* to print. Once again we caution you: don't confuse the value of the subscript with the value assigned to the subscripted variable.

DO IT

```
NEW

OK
5 REM-2ND SUBSCRIPTED VARIABLE DEMO
10 READ Y(0), Y(1), Y(2), Y(3)
20 FOR A=0 TO 3
30 ? "Y("; A; ") ="; Y(A)
40 NEXT A
60 DATA 3, 8, 2, 6.5
RUN
Y( 0 ) = 3
Y( 1 ) = 8
Y( 2 ) = 2
Y( 3 ) = 6.5

OK
```

READ

Our second demo used a FOR-NEXT loop to print subscripted variables and their assigned values. Now let's make the assignment of values to subscripted variables more automatic too. Our next demo program uses a FOR-NEXT loop to READ values from the DATA statement and assign them one at a time to a subscripted variable. The value of the FOR-NEXT loop control variable is used to decide which subscripted variable to assign the DATA value to in Line 20, and which subscripted variable and its value to PRINT in Line 30.

DO IT

```
NEW

OK
5 REM-3RD SUBSCRIPTED VARIABLE DEMO
10 FOR A=0 TO 10
20 READ Y(A)
30 ? "Y("; A; ") ="; Y(A)
40 NEXT A
50 DATA 3, 8, 2, 6.5, 211, 81, 1, -32, 7, .3333, 5
RUN
Y( 0 ) = 3
Y( 1 ) = 8
Y( 2 ) = 2
Y( 3 ) = 6.5
Y( 4 ) = 211
Y( 5 ) = 81
Y( 6 ) = 1
Y( 7 ) =-32
Y( 8 ) = 7
Y( 9 ) = .3333
Y( 10 ) = 5

OK
```

Now Let Me Make This Perfectly
CLEAR

Note that the value of A is the value of the FOR-NEXT loop control variable, which increases by 1 (one) each time through the loop. Therefore, the first time through the loop, A = 0 and Y(A) is Y(0). The READ statement then assigns the first value from the DATA statement, 3, to the box labelled Y(0).

Don't confuse the value of the FOR-NEXT loop control variable A with the value of the subscripted variable Y(A), which is assigned from the DATA statement. We're just using the value of control variable A to have the computer assign values to an *array* or *list* of subscripted variables, one after the other. The value of A determines which subscripted variable Y(0) to Y(10) is assigned the next value from the DATA statement. FOR-NEXT loops make it easy to assign a lot of values to a lot of variables, and subscripted variables make it easy to keep track of a lot of values.

A One Liner

Want to try that last little program in multiple statements per line?

Do it like this:

```
10 FOR A=0 TO 10 : READ Y(A) : ? "Y("; A; ") ="; Y(A) : NEXT A
20
30
40
LIST
```

After replacing line 10, just type the line numbers for lines you want to take out, and hit RETURN.

```
5 REM-3RD SUBSCRIPTED VARIABLE DEMO
10 FOR A=0 TO 10 : READ Y(A) : PRINT "Y("; A; ") ="; Y(A) : NEXT A
50 DATA 3, 8, 2, 6.5, 211, 81, 1, -32, 7, .3333, 5
OK
RUN
Y( 0 ) = 3
Y( 1 ) = 8
Y( 2 ) = 2
Y( 3 ) = 6.5
Y( 4 ) = 211
Y( 5 ) = 81
Y( 6 ) = 1
Y( 7 ) =-32
Y( 8 ) = 7
Y( 9 ) = .3333
Y( 10 ) = 5

OK
```

RUN IT — Same Old Results...

(Did you get the same output?)

THIS IS ONLY A TEST

Test your memory — do you remember that after a RUN of a program, all the values are still stored in the computer's memory? Well then, use direct mode to see if the values of the subscripted variables are really what the last program's output says they are.

```
? Y(3), Y(5), Y(10)
6.5          81           5
OK
```

Now, how about that. The values really are stored in boxes identified by subscripted variables.

(subscripted) string variables

String variables can have subscripts too. The only difference is that the string variable dollar sign ($) must come just before the subscript parentheses, like this: Y$(4). Let's use our trusty FOR-NEXT loop to assign strings from a DATA statement to a list of subscripted string variables, Y$(0) to Y$(6).

```
NEW          DO IT
OK
5 REM-SUBSCRIPTED STRING VARIABLE DEMO
10 FOR A=0 TO 6
20 READ Y$(A)
30 ? "Y$("; A; ") ="; Y$(A)
40 NEXT A
50 DATA APPLE, PEAR, PEACH, CHERRY, PLUM, MELON, GRAPE
RUN
Y$( 0 ) =APPLE
Y$( 1 ) =PEAR
Y$( 2 ) =PEACH
Y$( 3 ) =CHERRY
Y$( 4 ) =PLUM
Y$( 5 ) =MELON
Y$( 6 ) =GRAPE

OK
```

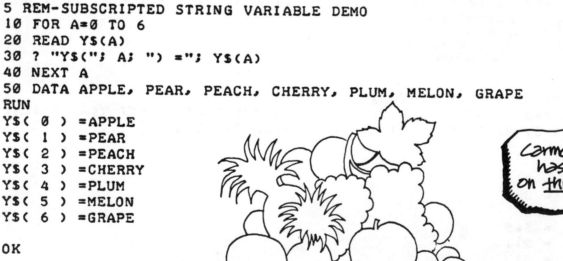

Carmen Miranda has nothing on _this_ program!

122

If you need further convincing, use direct mode to see which string is stored in which subscripted string variable.

```
? YS(2),  YS(4),  YS(0),  YS(3)
PEACH         PLUM          APPLE         CHERRY

OK
```

Be clear about this: different variables can be used to determine which subscripted variables is being referred to. It's the *value* of the variable used to indicate the subscript that is important. Do another direct mode statement to illustrate this point. (You haven't typed NEW have you? Well, don't!)

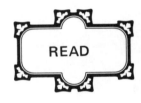

```
A=3 : B=3 : C=3 : ? YS(A), YS(B), YS(C)
CHERRY        CHERRY        CHERRY

OK
```

No matter what variable is used to tell the computer the value of the subscript, if the subscripted variable is Y$(3), then the computer will print the string assigned to Y$(3).

This just gets more and more interesting, and opens more and more programming possibilities. In order to determine the value of a subscript, the computer will even do calculations inside the subscript parentheses. Try it in direct mode, with our fruity list assigned to the Y$ subscripted variables still in the computers memory.

```
X=2 : Y=8 : Z=6 : ? YS(Y/X), YS(Z-X), YS((Y*Z)/(X*Z))
PLUM          PLUM          PLUM

OK
```

Hmmmm, it would seem that every one of those calculations in the subscript parentheses resulted in the same subscript value. Do you agree? Don't you wish this was a slot machine?

two loops

DO IT

Now let's use two different FOR-NEXT loops, one to READ the data into the subscripted variable boxes, and a different one to PRINT the contents of the subscripted variable boxes. If the last program is still in the computers memory (type LIST to make sure, if you wish), then you can avoid retyping the DATA statement by the following subterfuge.

Replace Line 10 like this:

```
10 FOR A=0 TO 6 : READ Y$(A) : NEXT A
```

Next replace Line 20 like this:

```
20 FOR B=0 TO 6 : ? Y$(B) : NEXT B
```

Take out Lines 30 and 40 by typing 30, then hitting RETURN, and then type 40 and hit RETURN. Remember, that eliminates those lines from the program by replacing those lines with ... nothing! Now LIST your revised program, note the changes, and RUN it.

```
30
40
LIST

5 REM-SUBSCRIPTED STRING VARIABLE DEMO
10 FOR A=0 TO 6 : READ Y$(A) : NEXT A
20 FOR B=0 TO 6 : PRINT Y$(B) : NEXT B
50 DATA APPLE, PEAR, PEACH, CHERRY, PLUM, MELON, GRAPE
OK
RUN
APPLE
PEAR
PEACH
CHERRY
PLUM
MELON
GRAPE

OK
```

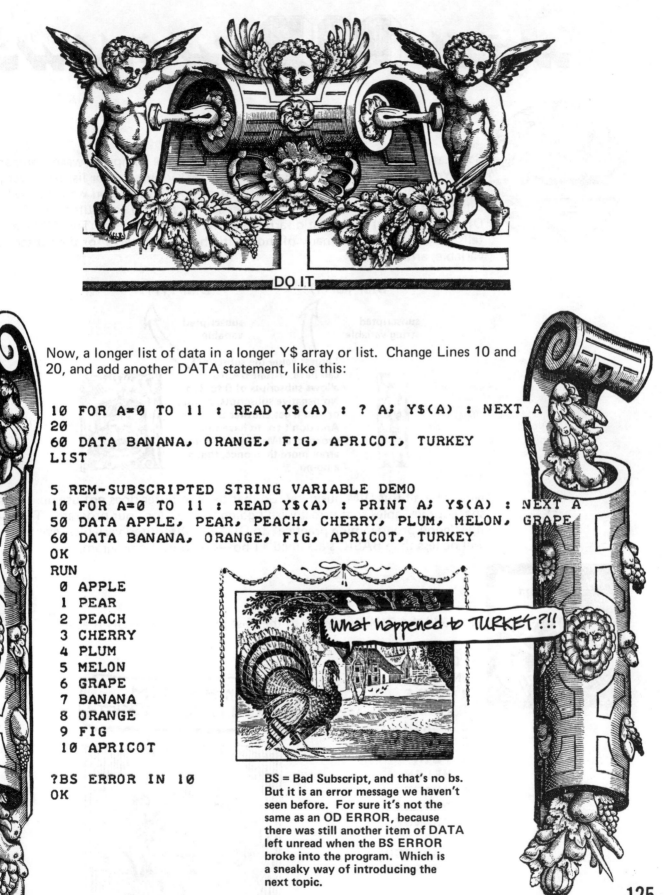

Now, a longer list of data in a longer Y$ array or list. Change Lines 10 and 20, and add another DATA statement, like this:

```
10 FOR A=0 TO 11 : READ Y$(A) : ? A; Y$(A) : NEXT A
20
60 DATA BANANA, ORANGE, FIG, APRICOT, TURKEY
LIST

5 REM-SUBSCRIPTED STRING VARIABLE DEMO
10 FOR A=0 TO 11 : READ Y$(A) : PRINT A; Y$(A) : NEXT A
50 DATA APPLE, PEAR, PEACH, CHERRY, PLUM, MELON, GRAPE
60 DATA BANANA, ORANGE, FIG, APRICOT, TURKEY
OK
RUN
 0 APPLE
 1 PEAR
 2 PEACH
 3 CHERRY
 4 PLUM
 5 MELON
 6 GRAPE
 7 BANANA
 8 ORANGE
 9 FIG
 10 APRICOT

?BS ERROR IN 10
OK
```

What happened to TURKEY?!!

BS = Bad Subscript, and that's no bs. But it is an error message we haven't seen before. For sure it's not the same as an OD ERROR, because there was still another item of DATA left unread when the BS ERROR broke into the program. Which is a sneaky way of introducing the next topic.

125

So what is a Bad Subscript? It is a subscript that the computer wasn't prepared for. You see, BASIC automatically assumes that your array or list of subscripted variables will have subscripts from 0 to 10 <u>at most</u>. But if you want to use larger subscripts, you have to tell the computer so. To tell the computer the DIMensions (size) of the list or array, use the DIM statement. The DIM statement tells the computer how many of those little boxes to reserve for the subscripted variable, array or list.

DIM Y$(11)　　　　　　DIM Y(11)

**subscripted
string variable**　　　　**subscripted
variable**

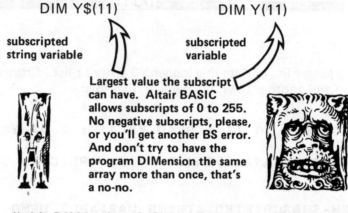

Largest value the subscript can have. Altair BASIC allows subscripts of 0 to 255. No negative subscripts, please, or you'll get another BS error. And don't try to have the program DIMension the same array more than once, that's a no-no.

Now why all this DIM business? So that the computer does not use up unnessary space for variables that it really isn't going to need for your program. They say it is "good programming practice" to DIM all subscripted variables, **even if** there will be less than BASIC's assumed 11 boxes used in the program.

DO IT

Now add the DIM statement to that last program, and RUN it again.

```
6 DIM Y$(11)
RUN
   0 APPLE
   1 PEAR
   2 PEACH
   3 CHERRY
   4 PLUM
   5 MELON
   6 GRAPE
   7 BANANA
   8 ORANGE
   9 FIG
  10 APRICOT
  11 TURKEY

OK
```

Thanks to DIM, we can have TURKEY!

It works just the same for values as for string arrays.

Now add a DIM statement and try the program again.

```
NEW

OK


10 FOR B=0 TO 15
20 F(B)=B
30 PRINT "F("; B; ") =";  F(B)
40 NEXT B
OK
RUN
F( 0  ) = 0
F( 1  ) = 1
F( 2  ) = 2
F( 3  ) = 3
F( 4  ) = 4
F( 5  ) = 5
F( 6  ) = 6
F( 7  ) = 7
F( 8  ) = 8
F( 9  ) = 9
F( 10 ) = 10

?BS ERROR IN 20
OK
```

```
5 DIM F(15)
RUN
F( 0  ) = 0
F( 1  ) = 1
F( 2  ) = 2
F( 3  ) = 3
F( 4  ) = 4
F( 5  ) = 5
F( 6  ) = 6
F( 7  ) = 7
F( 8  ) = 8
F( 9  ) = 9
F( 10 ) = 10
F( 11 ) = 11
F( 12 ) = 12
F( 13 ) = 13
F( 14 ) = 14
F( 15 ) = 15

OK
```

There's always one more thing to learn. Take out Line 20 in the last program, to see what values are stored in the F array if you don't assign any value.

```
20
LIST

5 DIM F(15)
10 FOR B=0 TO 15
30 PRINT "F("; B; ") =";  F(B)
40 NEXT B
OK
```

```
RUN
F( 0  ) = 0
F( 1  ) = 0
F( 2  ) = 0
F( 3  ) = 0
F( 4  ) = 0
F( 5  ) = 0
F( 6  ) = 0
F( 7  ) = 0
F( 8  ) = 0
F( 9  ) = 0
F( 10 ) = 0
F( 11 ) = 0
F( 12 ) = 0
F( 13 ) = 0
F( 14 ) = 0
F( 15 ) = 0

OK
```

BASIC assumes that any variable, including any subscripted variable, has a value of zero until it is told otherwise.

127

SIMULATED *Tumblin' Die*

One nice thing about having variables with subscripts is that the subscripts can be used to sort things (values or strings). At the same time a set of subscripted variables can count up things for us. Here is a little exercise in simulation. A simulation is an imitation of some real thing that might happen. Let's simulate the throwing of a die (that's one "dice"), and keep track of which face (number) comes up every time we throw it. We'll do this using D as the *subscript* of a subscripted variable. First, the ground work. Remember the RND function? (See page 77.)

```
30 D=INT(6*RND(1))+1
```

This will give us a simulated "throw of the die," that is, a random number between 1 and 6, just like rolling one of the 6 faces of a die. Next, remember how we used this program to count (See page 82.)

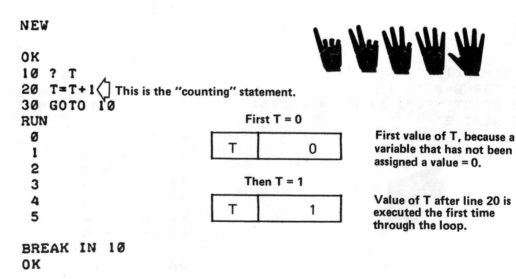

```
NEW

OK
10 ? T
20 T=T+1    ◁ This is the "counting" statement.
30 GOTO 10
RUN
 0
 1
 2
 3
 4
 5

BREAK IN 10
OK
```

First T = 0

T	0

First value of T, because a variable that has not been assigned a value = 0.

Then T = 1

T	1

Value of T after line 20 is executed the first time through the loop.

Using an Array to Keep Count

In our simulation program we will use the array T to keep track of how many 1's, 2's, 3's, 4's, 5's and 6's come up on our simulated die.

To begin with, all the values of the subscripted variable are 0.

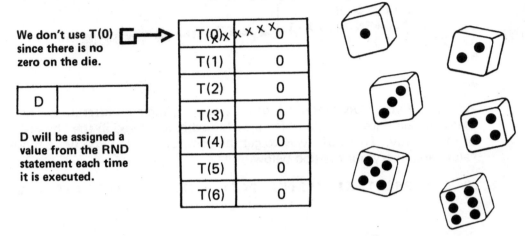

We don't use T(0) since there is no zero on the die.

T(0) x x x x x	0
T(1)	0
T(2)	0
T(3)	0
T(4)	0
T(5)	0
T(6)	0

D	

D will be assigned a value from the RND statement each time it is executed.

Let's say that the statement (shown on the previous page) that generates the RND integer gives us a 3, so that D = 3.

Each time D = 3 from the RND line, we want the value of T(3) to increase by one to show one roll of the number 3. We can use a "counting" statement with the T array subscripted variable, like this:

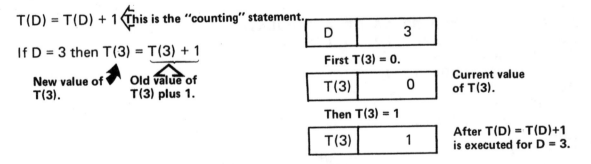

T(D) = T(D) + 1 ⟨This is the "counting" statement.

If D = 3 then T(3) = T(3) + 1

New value of T(3). Old value of T(3) plus 1.

D	3

First T(3) = 0.

T(3)	0

Current value of T(3).

Then T(3) = 1

T(3)	1

After T(D) = T(D)+1 is executed for D = 3.

But if D comes up a two (D = 2) then T(2) = T(2) + 1, that is, the value stored at T(2) is increased by 1.

Since there are 6 faces on the die with from 1 to 6 spots, we can use an array or list of 6 to keep track of what face comes up with each simulated throw of the die.

129

Now let's put together the pieces. First we have to tell the computer how many times to "roll the die."

```
5 REM-SIMULATED ROLLS OF A SIMULATED DIE
10 INPUT "HOW MANY ROLLS"; R
20 FOR K=1 TO R
30 D=INT(6*RND(1))+1
40 T(D)=T(D)+1
50 NEXT K
```

⟵⅃ This part counts the rolls.

All right, if you RUN that much of the program, the computer knows how many of each face came up in R rolls of the die, all stored in the "boxes" of the T array. Think of a way to get the computer to tell you what those values are, or try our method below.

```
60 FOR K=1 TO 6 : PRINT K; "'S:"; T(K) : NEXT K : PRINT : GOTO 10
```

Baby Needs a New Pair...

```
NEW

OK
5 REM-SIMULATED ROLLS OF A SIMULATED DIE
10 INPUT "HOW MANY ROLLS"; R
20 FOR K=1 TO R
30 D=INT(6*RND(1))+1
40 T(D)=T(D)+1
50 NEXT K
60 FOR K=1 TO 6 : ? K; "'S:"; T(K) : NEXT K : ? : GOTO 10
RUN
HOW MANY ROLLS? 500
   1 'S: 78
   2 'S: 90
   3 'S: 99
   4 'S: 80
   5 'S: 76
   6 'S: 77
```

◁K A short wait while the computer does 500 loops and tallies up (counts) the times each number 1 to 6 comes up when it "rolls the die." Even a computer doesn't do *that* many instructions in the bat of an eye.

```
HOW MANY ROLLS? 10000
   1 'S: 1671
   2 'S: 1835
   3 'S: 1833
   4 'S: 1735
   5 'S: 1693
   6 'S: 1733
```

◁K Time enough for a quick snack or a trip to the restroom while the computer does 10,000 loops, and executes the instructions inside the loop.

```
HOW MANY ROLLS?

OK
```

Circle Your Choice

READR) This way of using subscripted variables for counting things can be adapted to many kinds of record keeping. This same way of using subscripts is also a way of tabulating an opinion poll or questionaire, or to count votes, or to score an exam, or ... well, you think of some examples.

Say you want the computer to tabulate or count the responses to this questionaire. It could also be a voting ballot or the answers on a multiple choice test.

Which candidate will you vote for? (Circle the number for your choice.)
1. Need Some
2. Want More

Here are the votes (or whatever) in DATA statements.

```
900 DATA 1, 1, 1, 2, 1, 2, 1, 2, 2, 1, 2, 2, 2, 2, 1, 2, 1, 2
910 DATA 1, 2, 2, 2, 2, 1, 2, 1, 1, 1, 2, 2, 1, 1, 2, 1, 2, 2, 2
```

Let's have the computer READ them one at a time and have them tallied with our T array (kinda small array ... only two boxes, for a Vote of 1 or a Vote for 2).

```
10 READ V
```

```
30 T(V)=T(V)+1
```

T(1)	0
T(2)	0

The values are zero to start with.

V	

Value of V will change for each vote that is read from the DATA statement.

The new value of T(V) = old value of T(V) plus 1 for the vote being tallied. If READ V comes up with V = 1 from the DATA statement, then

$$T(V) = T(V) + 1$$
or $\quad T(1) = T(1) + 1$

The value in box

T(1)	

or

T(2)	

gets kicked up by +1, and to belabor the point, which one gets kicked depends on the value of the subscript V — whether V is 1 or 2 on that trip through the loop. (Pause here for inhalation therapy.)

After each vote is tallied, we want the computer to go back and READ another vote from the DATA statement.

```
40 GOTO 10
```

131

But let's say we want to know how many votes there were, but we want the computer to do the counting for us. Remember that BASIC doesn't know when to quit when it comes to READing votes (data) out of a DATA statement. So we need what is called a *flag* to tell the computer that it has reached the end of the data. Remember how it works? As the last item enetered in the last DATA statement, you stick on a value that is quite different from the others (or for string data, a code word). Then you put in an IF-THEN statement to check each value after it is read, to see if it is the flag value. Let's apply this to the vote sorting/counting program using −9999 as the flag.

```
10  READ V
20  IF V=-9999 THEN 50
30  T(V)=T(V)+1
40  GOTO 10

900 DATA 1, 1, 1, 2, 1, 2, 1, 2, 2, 1, 2, 2, 2, 2, 1, 2, 1, 2
910 DATA 1, 2, 2, 2, 2, 1, 2, 1, 1, 1, 2, 2, 1, 1, 2, 1, 2, 2, 2
920 DATA -9999
```

Now all we need is a way of having the computer tell us what it has counted.

```
50  ? "TOTAL VOTES:"; T(1)+T(2)
60  ? "CANDIDATE 1:"; T(1) : ? "CANDIDATE 2:"; T(2)
```

DO IT

So put it all together and RUN it.

```
LIST

10  READ V
20  IF V=-9999 THEN 50
30  T(V)=T(V)+1
40  GOTO 10
50  PRINT "TOTAL VOTES:"; T(1)+T(2)
60  PRINT "CANDIDATE 1:"; T(1) : PRINT "CANDIDATE 2:"; T(2)
900 DATA 1, 1, 1, 2, 1, 2, 1, 2, 2, 1, 2, 2, 2, 2, 1, 2, 1, 2
910 DATA 1, 2, 2, 2, 2, 1, 2, 1, 1, 1, 2, 2, 1, 1, 2, 1, 2, 2, 2
920 DATA -9999
OK
RUN
TOTAL VOTES: 37
CANDIDATE 1: 16
CANDIDATE 2: 21

OK
```

SALES REPORT

Here is a slightly different way of using a one dimensional array. We call the program Sales Report By Territory. Nationwide Peddlers has six sales territories, with one or more salespersons in each territory. Each salesperson in each territory submits a quarterly report (that's once every 3 months). We want a program to summarize the sales by territory, regardless of how many sales reports are submitted by the sellers in each of the six territories. Each sales report tells (1) which territory the report is from, numbered 1 to 6 and (2) how much was sold (in dollars) by the salesperson. Our DATA statements will hold pairs of DATA, with the first number indicating territory and the second number indicating sales in dollars.

```
100  DATA 1,2350,  4,1750,  2,2000,  1,1345,  5,3200,  3,1220,  6,2100
110  DATA 6,1240,  5,2450,  3,4200,  2,1275,  4,1100,  4,1800 ,3,900
120  DATA 5,2010,  2,1370,  1,1350,  5,1710,  3,2500,  -9999,-9999
```

Note the double "end of DATA" flags, because the computer will READ two values at a time, and we wouldn't want an Out of Data error, now would we?

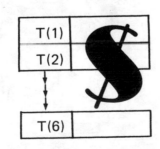

First we DIMension the T array, then READ S, D, where S = Sales territory number, and D is the Dollar sales for one salesperson in that territory. We use the subscript to sort the sales information by territory and keep track of the dollars in sales for each of the six sales territories (see Line 30).

```
5 REM-SALES REPORT BY TERRITORY
10 DIM T(6)
20 READ S,D : IF D=-9999 THEN 40
30 T(S)=T(S)+D : GOTO 20
```

Notice that T(1) keeps track of the sales in dollars for territory 1, T(2) keeps a tally of the sales in dollars for territory 2, and so on up to T(6).

The sales in Dollars for each territory (tallied by line 30) is the value of the subscripted variable T. But the number of the Sales territory determines the value of the subscript.

Now we want the computer to summarize the sales reports for us in a table of information. When the program is RUN, Lines 20 and 30 tally up the sales for each territory, with the subscript of T from 1 to 6 used to distinguish the territories. Next we need a heading for the sales report (Line 40). Then we need the territory number and the total sales made by all salespersons in that territory. A FOR-NEXT loop is the answer. The control variable is used to print the territory number, and to indicate which subscripted variable's value to PRINT (Line 50).

```
40 PRINT "TERRITORY", "SALES" : PRINT
50 FOR S=1 TO 6 : PRINT TAB(4); S, "$"; T(S) : NEXT S
```

And while we're at it, let's get a figure for the total sales in all territories. Since we haven't used T(0) for anything, we use it to add up all the sales recorded in T(1) to T(6).

Notice that we have used TAB twice in order to better position the output in this program.

```
60 PRINT "TOTAL SALES";
70 FOR S=1 TO 6 : T(0)=T(0)+T(S) : NEXT S : PRINT TAB(13); "$"; T(0)
```

DO IT

Now put it all together and RUN it, provided you understand how the program works.

```
NEW

OK


5 REM-SALES REPORT BY TERRITORY
10 DIM T(6)
20 READ S,D : IF D=-9999 THEN 40
30 T(S)=T(S)+D : GOTO 20
40 PRINT "TERRITORY", "SALES" : PRINT
50 FOR S=1 TO 6 : PRINT TAB(4); S, "$"; T(S) : NEXT S
60 PRINT "TOTAL SALES";
70 FOR S=1 TO 6 : T(0)=T(0)+T(S) : NEXT S : PRINT TAB(13); "$"; T(0)
100 DATA 1,2350, 4,1750, 2,2000, 1,1345, 5,3200, 3,1220, 6,2100
110 DATA 6,1240, 5,2450, 3,4200, 2,1275, 4,1100, 4,1800 ,3,900
120 DATA 5,2010, 2,1370, 1,1350, 5,1710, 3,2500, -9999,-9999
OK
RUN
TERRITORY       SALES

        1       $ 5045
        2       $ 4645
        3       $ 8820
        4       $ 4650
        5       $ 9370
        6       $ 3340
TOTAL SALES  $ 35870

OK
```

134

SALES AND SALARY REPORT

In the next program called Sales and Salary Report, we are using a kind of example, which in larger and more complete form, would be a typical business application of computers, and you know that there is a lot of computing done by businesses of all sizes these days. In the SSR program, we use 3 different subscripted variables, as well as several regular variables and even a string variable. The boxes for the subscripted variables hold information related to eight items that Diligent Industries is peddling through its hot sales force of four salespersons.

Each salesperson is selling the same 8 items. Each month the people on the sales force must each submit a report showing the quantity of each product or item sold. The monthly sales report could be a form like this:

Name _____			Branch Office _____				
Item	1	2	3	4	5	6	7	8
Sales								

Salesmen are paid a flat $700 per month plus 10% commission on sales over $3500 each month.

As sales manager, we want our computerized report to show: (1) the total sales in dollars for each salesperson and (2) each salesperson's total salary based on the flat salary plus commission. We also want (3) to show how many of each item or product was sold, and (4) the total dollar income from the sale of each item by all salespersons that month. We also want (5) the grand total of all salaries paid out and all income from sales of DI's great line of products.

SCORECARD

Well, you can't tell the variables without a scorecard, and here it is to assist you in figuring out how this program works and why.

P( ) — the price of the 8 items marketed by DI, which are entered into the subscripted variable boxes by Line 20, which READs the values into the P( ) list from the first DATA statement during 8 trips through the FOR-NEXT loop. Note that these prices for each item are the first 8 values in the DATA.

Q( ) — values are entered from the DATA statements, and the numbers stored in A( ) list are the quantity of each of the 8 items sold by one salesperson. This list is temporary, because the same Q( ) is used to show the quantity sold of the 8 items for each of the four salespersons (one at a time). See the loop from Line 90 to Line 100 or 110.

U( ) — Units sold — used to keep a tally of the number of each item sold regardless of which salesperson sold it. In otherwords, it keeps a tally of the information that is held for a time in the Q( ) list.

X — We use it as the FOR-NEXT loops (FOR X = 1 TO 8 ... NEXT) to READ in values from DATA statements, and to give the subscript location for those values, that is, P(X), Q(X), and U(X).

S — keeps a tally of S4 — the total sales in dollars for all salespersons.

S1 — keeps a tally of the total salaries paid out to all salespersons.

S2 — is the grand total of all sales in dollars.

S3 — is the salary of a salesperson if they sold over $3500 worth of items in this current monthly sales report.

S$ — keeps a tally of total sales for each salesperson, one at a time, so it has to be set back to zero after each salespersons sales have been figured (see Line 40), but it also tallies up the dollar value of the items sold (Line 80) and before it is set back to zero, the value tallied is added into S to get the total sales in dollars for the month.

N$ — used to hold the names of the salespersons for printing in the row summarizing their sales and salary, and READ from the DATA statement just before the item by item sales figures for the salesperson named.

THE VARIABLES

```
NEW

OK


10 DIM P(8), V(8), T(8), Q(8), N$(12)
20 FOR X=1 TO 8 : READ P(X) : NEXT X
30 PRINT "SALESPERSON", "TOTAL SALES", "SALARY"
40 S4=0
50 READ N$ : IF N$="END" THEN 120
60 FOR X=1 TO 8 : READ Q(X)
70 U(X)=U(X)+Q(X)
80 S4=S4 + Q(X)*P(X) : NEXT X
90 PRINT N$, S4,
100 S=S+S4 : IF S4<=700 THEN PRINT 700 : GOTO 40
110 S3=700+((S4-3500)*.1) : PRINT S3 : S1=S1+S3 : GOTO 40
120 PRINT : PRINT "TOTALS", S, S1 : PRINT
130 PRINT "ITEM", "PRICE/ITEM", "UNITS SOLD", "TOTAL SALES"
140 FOR X=1 TO 8 : PRINT X, P(X), U(X), U(X)*P(X)
150 S2=S2+U(X)*P(X) : NEXT X
160 PRINT : PRINT "GRAND TOTAL OF SALES",, S2
200 DATA 2.05, 18.45, 6.75, 9.95, 25.00, 16.50, 5.50, 12.60
210 DATA D.MILLER, 120, 15, 75, 0, 20, 100, 80, 144
220 DATA B.MIDLER, 160, 1, 90, 55, 16, 120, 96, 132
230 DATA P.PADRE, 80, 10, 60, 40, 5, 75, 10, 55
240 DATA A.XAVIER, 144, 60, 96, 96, 36, 144, 106, 90
250 DATA END
OK
RUN
```

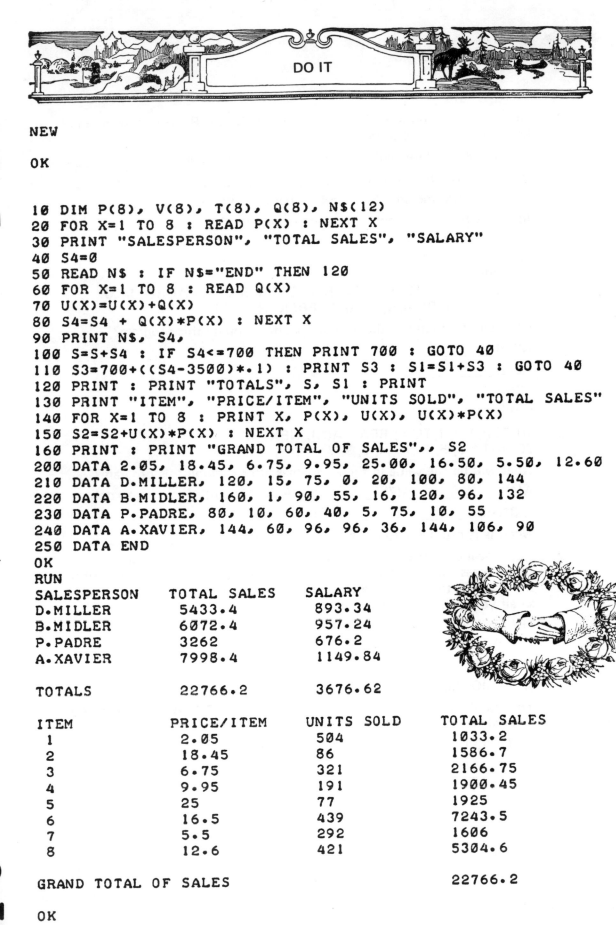

SALESPERSON	TOTAL SALES	SALARY
D.MILLER	5433.4	893.34
B.MIDLER	6072.4	957.24
P.PADRE	3262	676.2
A.XAVIER	7998.4	1149.84
TOTALS	22766.2	3676.62

ITEM	PRICE/ITEM	UNITS SOLD	TOTAL SALES
1	2.05	504	1033.2
2	18.45	86	1586.7
3	6.75	321	2166.75
4	9.95	191	1900.45
5	25	77	1925
6	16.5	439	7243.5
7	5.5	292	1606
8	12.6	421	5304.6

```
GRAND TOTAL OF SALES                        22766.2

OK
```

1. Answer these questions about the Sales and Salary Report program and listing found in this chapter.

    (a) In which statement are the units sold added together?_____

    (b) What is done in Line 90? _____

    (c) Line 100 includes S = S+S4. What does that do?_____

    (d) In which statement is the salary computed? _____

2. 5 FOR X = 1 TO 5
    10   READ A$(X), S(X)
    20   NEXT X
    30   DATA D. MILLER, 500, B. MIDLER, 950, P. PADRE, 1400
    40   DATA J. BLACK, 1500, L. FRENCH, 2000

    What will be found in these variables after running this program?

    A$(5) _____

    A$(2) _____

    S(3) _____

    S(1) _____

3. 10 FOR N = 1 TO 8; READ A(N): NEXT N
    20 DATA 3, 5, 2, 16, 4, 5, 9, 7

    What will be the value in these variables after running this program?

    A(4) _____ A(7) _____ A(A(1)+A(5)) _____ (watch it)
    A(3*A(3)) _____

4. When is it necessary to use a DIM statement? _____

5. Your local computer club asks you to prepare the program that will count votes for the upcoming officer election. Here is the ballot. Write the program to accumulate votes and print a nice report (do a nice job so all your fellow members will be impressed!).

    PRESIDENT   VICE PRESIDENT   TREASURER
    1.   A. ABLE ____   1.   M. MAC ____   1.   S. SOBER ____
    2.   B. BAKER ____   2.   J. ROVER ____   2.   T. MILSTON ____
    3.   C JONES ____   3.   M MANGI ____   3.   G GONIF ____

    You should place the results from each ballot in DATA statements like this:

    DATA 2, 1, 3, 3, 2, 3

6.	You have your school transcript in front of you. The college of your future choice says they will accept anyone with 75 A and B grades. Write a program to count your A's and B's. Place all your grades in DATA statements using this scale:

A = 4   B = 3   C = 2   D = 1   F(n/c) = 5

DATA 4, 3, 4, 2, 2, 1, 4, 3

7.	Slot machine simplified: The string array exercise in this chapter with cherries and plums, etc. sets up a natural situation for a slot machine simulation (Nevada style). Try to write a program that simulates a simple machine and as energy and interest allows, add to it to make it more sophisticated by fixing the odds, increasing the WIN chances, adding more money to the betting, etc.

Simple form: From DATA statements read in to an array: CHERRY, BAR, PEACH, PLUM, APPLE. Then choose three of them randomly and print the results.

If column 1 is a cherry, you win $0.05.
If column 1 and 2 are the same you win $0.10.
If column 1, 2 and 3 are the same you win $0.25.
If columns 1, 2, and 3 are BAR, you win whatever is in the "kitty."

2-Count 'em-2

READ

If you've been roaring through this book, now might be a good time for a breather. It is important that you feel a comfortable understanding of subscripted variables. Have you tried the example programs? Do you understand how subscripted variables store values? Have you tried out any ideas of your own that use subscripted variables? If you need to review, now is the time, because we're about to hit you with an expanded form of subscripted variables.

Up to now, we have used subscripted variables such as P(8) and T(D). These are singly subscripted variables. That is, each variable has exactly one subscript.

$$P(8) \qquad T(D) \qquad Y\$(X)$$

Just one

Now we have a new one to spring on you, *doubly subscripted variables*, variables that have two subscripts.

$$P(2,3) \qquad Y\$(2,5) \qquad T(A,B)$$

Two subscripts.

The subscripts are separated with a *comma*. An easy way to think about doubly subscripted variables is with those little boxes arranged in an *array* of rows and columns, like this:

Presenting our doubly subscripted variable   A(4,3)

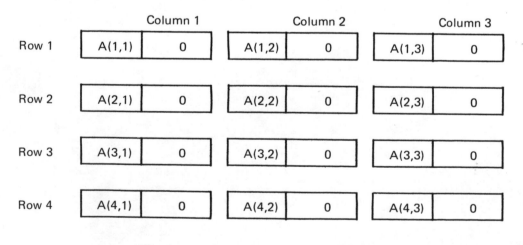

	Column 1	Column 2	Column 3
Row 1	A(1,1) 0	A(1,2) 0	A(1,3) 0
Row 2	A(2,1) 0	A(2,2) 0	A(2,3) 0
Row 3	A(3,1) 0	A(3,2) 0	A(3,3) 0
Row 4	A(4,1) 0	A(4,2) 0	A(4,3) 0

140

A(4,3)

Row
Column

The boxes show that all the values assigned to the variables in this two-dimensional array are zero.

This stacked up arrangement allows us to relate subscripts to particular locations or "boxes" for holding values in rows and columns. Want some vocabulary? The rectangular arrangement of doubly subscripted variables in rows and columns is called a *table* or *matrix*, or *two-dimensional array*. Remember that an array of singly subscripted variables is a *list* or *one-dimensional array*.

This is a list or a one-dimensional array. ⟹

B(0)	
B(1)	
B(2)	
B(3)	

One subscript, one dimension.

2-D

This is a table or two-dimensional array: ⟱

A(0,0)		A(0,1)		A(0,2)		A(0,3)		A(0,4)		A(0,5)	
A(1,0)		A(1,1)		A(1,2)		A(1,3)		A(1,4)		A(1,5)	
A(2,0)		A(2,1)		A(2,2)		A(2,3)		A(2,4)		A(2,5)	
A(3,0)		A(3,1)		A(3,2)		A(3,3)		A(3,4)		A(3,5)	
A(4,0)		A(4,1)		A(4,2)		A(4,3)		A(4,4)		A(4,5)	

Two subscripts
Two dimensions

Just as for singly subscripted variables, those with two subscripts can have subscripts starting at zero. Up to 30 values or strings may be assigned to this particular array, each identified by its own subscripted variable. Of course, if it were a string array, there would be a $ after the A's like this: A$(3,4).

Arrays created by using variables with double subscripts are handy for storing data in the computer. You *must* tell the computer what the maximum DIMensions of your doubly subscripted variables will be. You may use the same DIM statement to dimension all variables in one statement, whether string variables, singly or doubly subscripted variables:

20 DIM C(3,4), X$(15), Y(12), M$(F,S)

line number ↑   2 dim array   1 dim string array   1 dim array   2 dim string array

Are you getting the idea? A doubly subscripted variable is simply the name of a box or location in the computer where you can store a value or a string, just like the other variables you have used. Just as a singly subscripted variable may have a variable as a subscript, a doubly subscripted variable may have both its subscripts as variables, or even expressions to be calculated.

Of course, the computer must have some way of knowing the value of variables used as subscripts. For practice, fill in the blanks for the subscripted variables in the boxes, with the subscript *values*.

$B(K,2) = 365$

$K = 8$

K	8
B(__ ,2)	365

↖ K

$C(R,C) = 4$

$R = 0$

$C = 3$

R	0
C	3
C(__ , __)	4

↖R   ↖C

Note that the single numeric variable C is different from the subscripted variable C(R,C).

$F\$(N-1, K*2) = \text{"HOT"}$

$N = 3$

$K = 2$

N	3
K	2
F$(__ , __)	HOT

↖N-1   ↖K*2

DOUBLE DOUBLE SUBSCRIPT DEMO

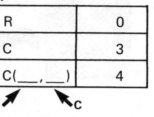

```
NEW

OK
5 REM-DOUBLE SUBSCRIPT DEMO
10 DIM C(2,3)
20 READ C(0,0), C(0,1), C(0,2), C(0,3)
30 READ C(1,0), C(1,1), C(1,2), C(1,3)
40 READ C(2,0), C(2,1), C(2,2), C(2,3)
50 ? C(0,0), C(0,1), C(0,2), C(0,3)
60 ? C(1,0), C(1,1), C(1,2), C(1,3)
70 ? C(2,0), C(2,1), C(2,2), C(2,3)
100 DATA 5, 10, 88, -19, 100, 8.25, 91, 22, -1.5, 15, 9, 2
RUN
 5           10          88          -19
 100         8.25        91          22
-1.5         15          9           2

OK
```

142

Now fill in the values assigned to these subscripted variables by the last program. We did the first two.

C(0,0)	5	C(0,1)	10	C(0,2)		C(0,3)	
C(1,0)		C(1,1)		C(1,2)		C(1,3)	
C(2,0)		C(2,1)		C(2,2)		C(2,3)	

Now let's start automating. As we did with one-dimensional arrays before, we use FOR-NEXT loops to give values to the subscripts, and thus tell the computer which subscripted variable it is to deal with. But now we have 2 subscripts, so we use *nested* FOR-NEXT loops to go through the possible values.

Replace Lines 50, 60, and 70 in the last program, and add Line 80.

```
50 FOR R=0 TO 2
60 FOR C=0 TO 3
70 ? "C("; R; ","; C; ") ="; C(R,C); "    ";
80 NEXT C : ? : NEXT R
LIST

5 REM-DOUBLE SUBSCRIPT DEMO
10 DIM C(2,3)
20 READ C(0,0), C(0,1), C(0,2), C(0,3)
30 READ C(1,0), C(1,1), C(1,2), C(1,3)
40 READ C(2,0), C(2,1), C(2,2), C(2,3)
50 FOR R=0 TO 2
60 FOR C=0 TO 3
70 PRINT "C("; R; ","; C; ")="; C(R,C); "    ";
80 NEXT C : PRINT : NEXT R
100 DATA 5, 10, 88, -19, 100, 8.25, 91, 22, -1.5, 15, 9, 2
OK
```

```
80 NEXT C : ? : NEXT R
```
Used to "cancel" the ; at the end of Line 70 and start a new line of output.

Did you have trouble entering Line 70 correctly? Let's look at it more closely.

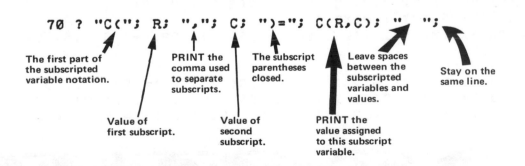

```
70 ? "C("; R; ","; C; ")="; C(R,C); "    ";
```

The first part of the subscripted variable notation.

Value of first subscript.

PRINT the comma used to separate subscripts.

Value of second subscript.

The subscript parentheses closed.

PRINT the value assigned to this subscript variable.

Leave spaces between the subscripted variables and values.

Stay on the same line.

Now RUN the program.

```
RUN
C( 0 , 0 )= 5    C( 0 , 1 )= 10   C( 0 , 2 )= 88    C( 0 , 3 )=-19
C( 1 , 0 )= 100    C( 1 , 1 )= 8.25   C( 1 , 2 )= 91    C( 1 , 3 )= 22
C( 2 , 0 )=-1.5    C( 2 , 1 )= 15   C( 2 , 2 )= 9   C( 2 , 3 )= 2

OK
```

Well, I suppose you have guessed it. The next step is to automate the assignment of values to variables with double subscripts. So let's modify the program again, to automatically go through the C array and assign values to all those subscripted variables.

DO IT

Replace Lines 20, 30 and 40 with these nested FOR-NEXT loops.

```
20 FOR R=0 TO 2 : FOR C=0 TO 3
30 READ C(R,C)
40 NEXT C,R
LIST

5 REM-DOUBLE SUBSCRIPT DEMO
10 DIM C(2,3)
20 FOR R=0 TO 2 : FOR C=0 TO 3
30 READ C(R,C)
40 NEXT C,R
50 FOR R=0 TO 2
60 FOR C=0 TO 3
70 PRINT "C("; R; ","; C; ")="; C(R,C); "   ";
80 NEXT C : PRINT : NEXT R
100 DATA 5, 10, 88, -19, 100, 8.25, 91, 22, -1.5, 15, 9, 2
OK
RUN
C( 0 , 0 )= 5    C( 0 , 1 )= 10   C( 0 , 2 )= 88    C( 0 , 3 )=-19
C( 1 , 0 )= 100    C( 1 , 1 )= 8.25   C( 1 , 2 )= 91    C( 1 , 3 )= 22
C( 2 , 0 )=-1.5    C( 2 , 1 )= 15   C( 2 , 2 )= 9   C( 2 , 3 )= 2

OK
```

SUPERTALLY

Let's go back to our vote counting program. Using variables with double subscripts allows us to add another dimension to tally or count up for us. Our new questionaire asks "Who did you vote for in the last election?"

Question 1: Who did you vote for in the last election? Circle the number by your choice.	Question 2: Circle the number by your age group.
1. Powerman	1. 18 – 29
2. Moneyman	2. 30 – 39
3. Other	3. 40 – 49
	4. 50 or over

We want to write a program to summarize the data gathered from this poll. Note that there are two questions, and 3 possible answers for the first, and 4 possible answers for the second. Any one questionaire yeilds two answers, the answer to Question 1 (which can be a 1, 2 or 3), and the answer to Question 2 (which can be a 1, 2, 3, or 4.) Obviously we want to know the answers as related to age groups, as well as the totals of votes in each catagory from Question 1 for all age groups, just like the big time pollsters. (Gallup Poll has nothing on us!)

Remember how we used the subscript of a variable to decide which catagory to tally a vote in?

```
10 READ V
30 T(V)=T(V)+1
```

T(1)	
T(2)	

Now we have two answers to tally, so we use a two dimensional array.

	18 – 29	30 – 39	40 – 49	50 or over
Powerman	C(1,1)	C(1,2)	C(1,3)	C(1,4)
Moneyman	C(2,1)	C(2,2)	C(2,3)	C(2,4)
Other	C(3,1)	C(3,2)	C(3,3)	C(3,4)

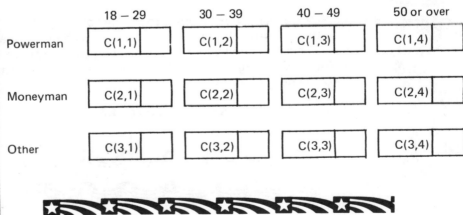

Since there are two questions, our DATA for each reply consists of two numbers—the answer to Question 1 (we use V for Vote) and the answer to Question 2 (we use A for Age group).

There are 12 possible combinations of answers. A vote of 1 (for Powerman) by someone in age group 1 (18 — 29) gives us this pair of answers: 1,1. A vote of 3 (for Other) by someone in age group 2 (30 — 39) gives us this pair of answers: 3,2. Are you beginning to see how a doubly-subscripted variable in array C(V,A) can be used to tally the 12 possible combinations of answers to the questionaire?

Since there are 3 possible answers to Question 1, and 4 possible age catagories for each respondent, we need a 3 by 4 array, and we'll start off the program with a DIM statement.

```
10 DIM C(3,4)
```

We will READ V,A from DATA statements. Just to help make things clear, we have the responses to the questionaires coded by number in pairs in the DATA statements. Here are the replies to our questionaire. Remember, each reply is a pair of numbers.

```
900 DATA 1,2, 1,3, 2,2, 2,3, 2,1, 3,2, 3,4, 2,3, 2,3, 3,2, 1,4
910 DATA 3,1, 3,2, 1,4, 2,4, 2,3, 1,3, 2,4, 1,4, 2,2
920 DATA 2,1, 2,2, 3,2, 2,4, 1,2, 1,3, 2,4, 1,4, 2,3, 3,1, 3,3
```

We need a flag to signal the end of the DATA. However, since we are reading two values at a time (READ V,A) from the DATA, we need two flags so that the computer will not give us an OD ERROR message. Also we need a statement to check for the flag, and tell the computer where to branch to if it has finished reading all the DATA.

```
20 READ V,A : IF A=-9999 THEN 40
930 DATA -9999, -9999
```

Naturally we want the computer to do the counting. So we need a statement telling the computer to tally the response to each questionaire in the box for the proper subscripted variable. Remember, each response is a *pair* of answers, the Vote and the Age group. Then we want the computer to branch back and READ the next pair of values.

```
30 C(V,A)=C(V,A)+1 : GOTO 20
```

146

So far, this much of the program (plus the DATA statements) will count all the responses to the questionaire.

```
LIST

5 REM-VOTE COUNTING WITH TWO-DIMENSIONAL ARRAY
10 DIM C(3,4)
20 READ V,A : IF A=-9999 THEN 40
30 C(V,A)=C(V,A)+1 : GOTO 20
900 DATA 1,2, 1,3, 2,2, 2,3, 2,1, 3,2, 3,4, 2,3, 2,3, 3,2, 1,4
910 DATA 3,1, 3,2, 1,4, 2,4, 2,3, 1,3, 2,4, 1,4, 2,2
920 DATA 2,1, 2,2, 3,2, 2,4, 1,2, 1,3, 2,4, 1,4, 2,3, 3,1, 3,3
930 DATA -9999, -9999
OK
```

The next section of the program must tell the computer to tell us what it has counted. We want the following information when the program is RUN.

```
RUN
```

CANDIDATE	18-29	30-39	40-49	50 +
POWERMAN	0	2	3	4
MONEYMAN	2	3	5	4
OTHER	2	4	1	1

```
OK
```

First a statement to print the headings and a blank line.

```
40 ? "CANDIDATE", "18-29", "30-39", "40-49", "50 +" : ?
```

And now the information stored in the C array. If you guessed that we will use nested FOR-NEXT loops, you are as brilliant as you look. But what about the candidates' names? Let's put those in a DATA statement, and assign them to a string variable, C$. If we place the READ C$: PRINT C$ instructions *inside* the first loop, but *before* the second loop, they will be printed at the beginning of each line in the table. See page 00.

```
50 FOR V=1 TO 3 : READ C$ : ? C$,
60 FOR A=1 TO 4 : ? C(V,A), : NEXT A,V
940 DATA POWERMAN, MONEYMAN, OTHER
```

147

Now put it all together and RUN it.

```
LIST

5 REM-VOTE COUNTING WITH TWO-DIMENSIONAL ARRAY
10 DIM C(3,4)
20 READ V,A : IF A=-9999 THEN 40
30 C(V,A)=C(V,A)+1 : GOTO 20
40 PRINT "CANDIDATE", "18-29", "30-39", "40-49", "50 +" : PRINT
50 FOR V=1 TO 3 : READ C$ : PRINT C$,
60 FOR A=1 TO 4 : PRINT C(V,A), : NEXT A,V
900 DATA 1,2, 1,3, 2,2, 2,3, 2,1, 3,2, 3,4, 2,3, 2,3, 3,2, 1,4
910 DATA 3,1, 3,2, 1,4, 2,4, 2,3, 1,3, 2,4, 1,4, 2,2
920 DATA 2,1, 2,2, 3,2, 2,4, 1,2, 1,3, 2,4, 1,4, 2,3, 3,1, 3,3
930 DATA -9999, -9999
940 DATA POWERMAN, MONEYMAN, OTHER
OK
RUN
```

CANDIDATE	18-29	30-39	40-49	50 +
POWERMAN	0	2	3	4
MONEYMAN	2	3	5	4
OTHER	2	4	1	1

OK

READ

Let's get a little more information out of this collection of data. Let's have the computer give us the totals for each of the three answers to Question 1 regardless of age group.

Since we have not used the subscript zero in the doubly subscripted variable C(V,A), we have those "boxes" still free to hold information for us. So we will use C(1,0), C(2,0) and C(3,0) to tally up the votes or answers to each choice in Question 1 regardless of age group. Note that we use the FOR variable V to print which of the three choices in being reported to us (Line 80).

We could have *added* another DATA statement identical to 940, and used READ C$: PRINT C$ as in Line 50. We leave the choice up to you.

DO IT

Add these lines to the previous program and RUN the new version.

```
70 ? : ? "TOTALS:"
80 FOR V=1 TO 3 : ? "ANSWER"; V; ":";
90 FOR A=1 TO 4 : C(V,0)=C(V,0)+C(V,A) : NEXT A
100 ? C(V,0) : NEXT V
RUN
```

CANDIDATE	18-29	30-39	40-49	50 +
POWERMAN	0	2	3	4
MONEYMAN	2	3	5	4
OTHER	2	4	1	1

```
TOTALS:
ANSWER 1 : 9
ANSWER 2 : 14
ANSWER 3 : 8

OK
```

148

There is one more peice of information that we might want to have reported: the total number of people answering the questionaire. Let's just add on one more little program segment. Again we take advantage of the fact that we haven't used all the locations of the C(V,A) array with zero as subscript. To tally the C(V,0) values and store the total number of respondents to our poll, in C(0,0), we use anosther FOR-NEXT loop.

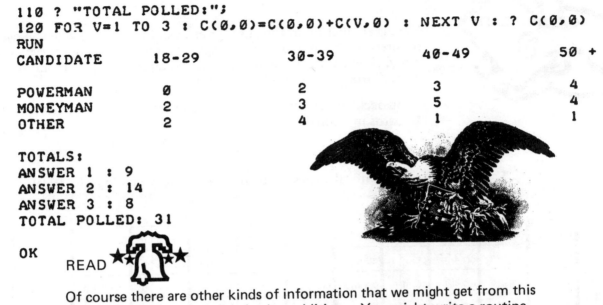

```
110 ? "TOTAL POLLED:";
120 FOR V=1 TO 3 : C(0,0)=C(0,0)+C(V,0) : NEXT V : ? C(0,0)
RUN
```

CANDIDATE	18-29	30-39	40-49	50 +
POWERMAN	0	2	3	4
MONEYMAN	2	3	5	4
OTHER	2	4	1	1

```
TOTALS:
ANSWER 1 : 9
ANSWER 2 : 14
ANSWER 3 : 8
TOTAL POLLED: 31

OK
READ
```

Of course there are other kinds of information that we might get from this data and our program, with further additions. You might write a routine (program segment) to tally how many people in each age group was polled. If you know statistics, you might try writing some routines to provide a statistical analysis of the program, or percentages in the various catagories. Use your imagination plus the knowledge of BASIC that you have worked on hard to learn.

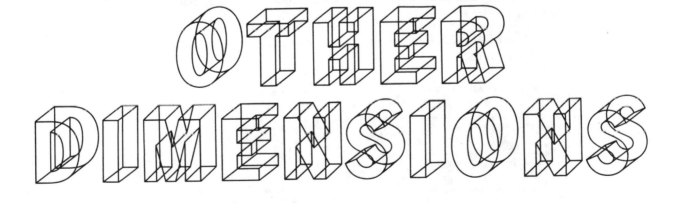

OTHER DIMENSIONS

Other Dimensions

You don't have to stop with 2 dimensional arrays. In fact, Altair BASIC allows up to 255 dimensions.

However, because of the limitations on the size of a statement line, you can't get much more than 34 dimensions into a statement.

DEAL ME IN!

READ

Here is another interesting use for arrays. In this case, when an event has occurred in the program, the computer "marks" the appropriate box in an array. This next programming project is a program that randomly "deals a card" from a deck of playing cards.

"The deck" is actually a 4 by 13 array with a box representing each of the 13 cards in 4 suits.

The Array D(4,13), with all values set to zero, as at the beginning of a RUN.

C(1,1) 0	C(1,2) 0	C(1,3) 0	C(1,4) 0	C(1,5) 0	C(1,6) 0	C(1,7) 0	C(1,8) 0	C(1,9) 0	C(1,10) 0	C(1,11) 0	C(1,12) 0	C(1,13) 0
C(2,1) 0	C(2,2) 0	C(2,3) 0	C(2,4) 0	C(2,5) 0	C(2,6) 0	C(2,7) 0	C(2,8) 0	C(2,9) 0	C(2,10) 0	C(2,11) 0	C(2,12) 0	C(2,13) 0
C(3,1) 0	C(3,2) 0	C(3,3) 0	C(3,4) 0	C(3,5) 0	C(3,6) 0	C(3,7) 0	C(3,8) 0	C(3,9) 0	C(3,10) 0	C(3,11) 0	C(3,12) 0	C(3,13) 0
C(4,1) 0	C(4,2) 0	C(4,3) 0	C(4,4) 0	C(4,5) 0	C(4,6) 0	C(4,7) 0	C(4,8) 0	C(4,9) 0	C(4,10) 0	C(4,11) 0	C(4,12) 0	C(4,13) 0

When the program is RUN, the computer "marks" the right box in the array with a −1 to show that the card has been dealt, and then prints the card and suit. We will have our program deal five cards, such as a poker hand.

The variables:

H   the FOR-NEXT line control variable to count to five for dealing five cards.

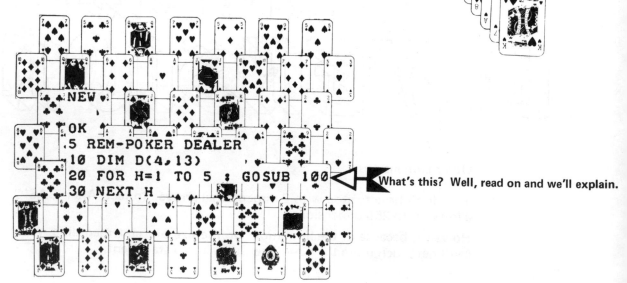

```
NEW
OK
5 REM-POKER DEALER
10 DIM D(4,13)
20 FOR H=1 TO 5 : GOSUB 100
30 NEXT H
```

What's this? Well, read on and we'll explain.

150

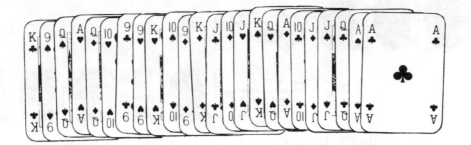

D(4,13)   the subscripted variable to keep track of which cards have been dealt by checking and "marking" in an array, so that the computer will not deal the same card twice. There are 13 cards in 4 suits — note the subscripts in the array D(4,13). The value of the subscripts are determined by two RND numbers, and that is how the computer will know which card is being dealt.

J   the suit of the card to be dealt (See Line 110).

K   the number (1 to 13 of the card to be dealt. See Line 100.

```
99 REM-CARD DEALING SUBROUTINE, LINES 100-330
100 K=INT(13*RND(1))+1
110 J=INT(4*RND(1))+1
120 IF D(J,K)=-1 THEN 100
130 D(J,K)=-1
```

In Line 130, the values of J and K determine which D(J,K) box will be marked or set to −1. We could have used any value other than zero to indicate that a particular box has been changed from zero. But before the box is marked −1, the computer checks to see if that "card" has already been dealt, that is, if the box for D(J,K) was already makred with a −1. Line 120 sends the computer back to try again with another set of RND numbers if there was already a −1 marked in the box.

In this program, each card has a number for its face value, "selected" at random from 1 to 13 by Line 100.

```
100 K=INT(13*RND(1))+1
```

Number:	1	2	3	4	5	6	7	8	9	10	11	12	13
Card:	Ace	2	3	4	5	6	7	8	9	10	JACK	QUEEN	KING

Each card has a number (1 to 4) for its suit, selected at random by Line 110.

```
110 J=INT(4*RND(1))+1
```

Number:	1	2	3	4
Suit:	clubs	spades	hearts	diamonds

Line 120 checks to make sure that card D(J,K) hasn't been dealt, and if it hasn't, Line 130 notes with a −1 that it is about to deal card D(J,K).

```
5 REM-POKER DEALER
10 DIM D(4,13)
20 FOR H=1 TO 5 : GOSUB 100
30 NEXT H
```

The main action in the program (Lines 100 to 330) is executed 5 times, in order to deal 5 cards. Here is the rest of the *subroutine* that deals or prints the cards.

subroutine

```
99 REM-CARD DEALING SUBROUTINE, LINES 100-330
100 K=INT(13*RND(1))+1
110 J=INT(4*RND(1))+1
120 IF D(J,K)=-1 THEN 100
130 D(J,K)=-1
140 ON K GOTO 200,210,210,210,210,210,210,210,210,210,220,230,240
150 ON J GOTO 300,310,320,330
200 ? " ACE "; : GOTO 150
210 ? K; : GOTO 150
220 ? " JACK "; : GOTO 150
230 ? " QUEEN "; : GOTO 150
240 ? " KING "; : GOTO 150
300 ? "OF CLUBS" : RETURN
310 ? "OF SPADES" : RETURN
320 ? "OF HEARTS" : RETURN
330 ? "OF DIAMONDS" : RETURN
```

We use the GOSUB statement to "call" the "card dealing subroutine" in the program, Lines 100 to 330. The GOSUB statement is *between* the FOR and the NEXT statements (Lines 10 and 20). This has the effect of sticking the *card dealing subroutine* part of the program between the FOR and NEXT statements, and in our program, that means that the subroutine is "called" and executed 5 times during the 5 trips through the FOR-NEXT loop.

GOSUB must be followed by a <u>line number</u> (just like the GO TO statement) that tells the computer where the subroutine starts. The computer <u>GO</u>es to the <u>SUB</u>routine that begins at the line indicated, and keeps RUNning the program statement by statement, until it comes to a RETURN statement.

Like FOR and NEXT, and READ and DATA, the GOSUB statement must <u>always</u> have a matching RETURN statement. RETURN is always the <u>last</u> statement in a subroutine. The RETURN statement tells the computer that it has finished the subroutine, and to RETURN to the next *line* in the program after the GOSUB statement. Therefore, the GOSUB (as well as the RETURN statement) must always be the <u>last</u> statement in a line with multiple statements. It happens that our card dealing subroutine can end at any of four different statements (Lines 300 — 330), so in this particular case the computer will RETURN to the line <u>after</u> the GOSUB statement after it has executed any one of the four statements on Lines 300 to 330.

But notice we were careful not to put the Line 30 NEXT H on the same line as the GOSUB statement. If we had, it would have missed the NEXT H statement when it RETURNed.

ON...GOTO...

Lines 140 and 150 introduce the ON ... GOTO statement.

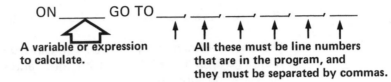

ON _____ GO TO ___, ___, ___, ___, ___,

A variable or expression to calculate.

All these must be line numbers that are in the program, and they must be separated by commas.

As many line numbers as can fit in a statement line, can follow an ON ...GOTO statement. If the ON ... GOTO variable is 1, then the computer *GO*es *TO* the first line number. If the variable value is 2, then it goes to the second line number listed, and so on. However, if the value of the ON ... GOTO variable is negative, or is zero, *OR* is begger than the number of line numbers after GOTO, then the computer just skips on ("falls through the statement," they say) to the next line numbered statement in the program.

This is handy, because you may wish to use more line numbers then will fit in one line. The trick is this: Say that only the first 10 line numbers in Line 140 actually fit on the line —

```
140 ON K GOTO 200,210,210,210,210,210,210,210,210,210
```

We left off the last 3 lines numbers, pretending they wouldn't fit. We tell our next ON ... GOTO variable to pick up where the last one left off, like this:

```
145 ON K-10 GOTO 220,230,240
```

Subtract the largest possible value of K for the last line. K would have to be greater than 10 in order to "fall through" the last statement and arrive at this line.

Like GOSUB and RETURN, ON ... GOTO must be the last statement if used in a multiple statement line, or else it must stand alone.

In Line 140 we find

```
140 ON K GOTO 200,210,210,210,210,210,210,210,210,210,220,230,240
```

This line selects which statement will be used to PRINT the card selected. If K = 1, then the computer goes to Line 200 and prints ACE. If K = 2, 3, 4, 5, 6, 7, 8, 9, or 10, then the computer is sent to Line 210 and prints the value of K (the number of the card being dealt). If K= 11, 12, or 13, the computer goes to Lines 220, 230 or 240 and prints JACK, QUEEN, or KING.

Notice that ON ... GOTO can sometimes substitute for bunches of IF...THEN statements.

The ON ... GOTO statement in Line 150 selects the name of the suit to be printed. We sure got double duty out of those RND value for J and K, didn't we?

153

DEAL ME OUT

One more refinement, and then you can try out the program. These statements go *after* the FOR ... NEXT loop, and are *not* part of the GOSUB 100 card dealing subroutine.

```
40 ? : INPUT "ANOTHER HAND, SAME DECK"; A$ : IF A$="YES" THEN 20
50 ? : INPUT "ANOTHER HAND, NEW DECK"; A$ : IF A$="NO" THEN END
60 FOR J=1 TO 4 : FOR K=1 TO 13 : D(J,K)=0 : NEXT K,J : GOTO 20
```

Line 60 is executed *only* if the answer to "ANOTHER HAND, SAME DECK" is not YES (IF ... THEN condition false), and if the answer to "ANOTHER HAND, NEW DECK" is not NO (IF ... THEN condition false).

Then Line 60 uses nested FOR-NEXT loops to set all the values in the D array back to zero.

Last minute notes on GOSUB.

You may have subroutines within subroutines, that is, GOSUB's inside of GOSUB's, just like nested FOR-NEXT loops. The first RETURN statement that is encountered RETURNs the program to the line after the last GOSUB statement executed. Makes sense, no? As another tidbit of knowledge, we should inform you that the ON ... GOTO statement has a close cousin, the ON ... GOSUB statement. We could have used it in the card dealing program replacing the following lines:

```
140 ON K GOSUB 200,210,210,210,210,210,210,210,210,210,220,230,240
200 ? " ACE "; : RETURN
210 ? K; : RETURN
220 ? " JACK "; : RETURN
230 ? " QUEEN "; : RETURN
240 ? " KING "; : RETURN
```

For this program, it is just like having a subroutine within a subroutine, except that the ON ... GOSUB statement was used in the "inside" subroutine. No matter which line the ON K GOSUB ... sends the computer to, it will RETURN to Line 150 (the line after the last GOSUB), because we have placed a RETURN command at the end of all the lines that the GOSUB could go to.

Now that the way this program works is crystal clear (better re-read if it isn't, and check the explanations with the program), go ahead and RUN it.

154

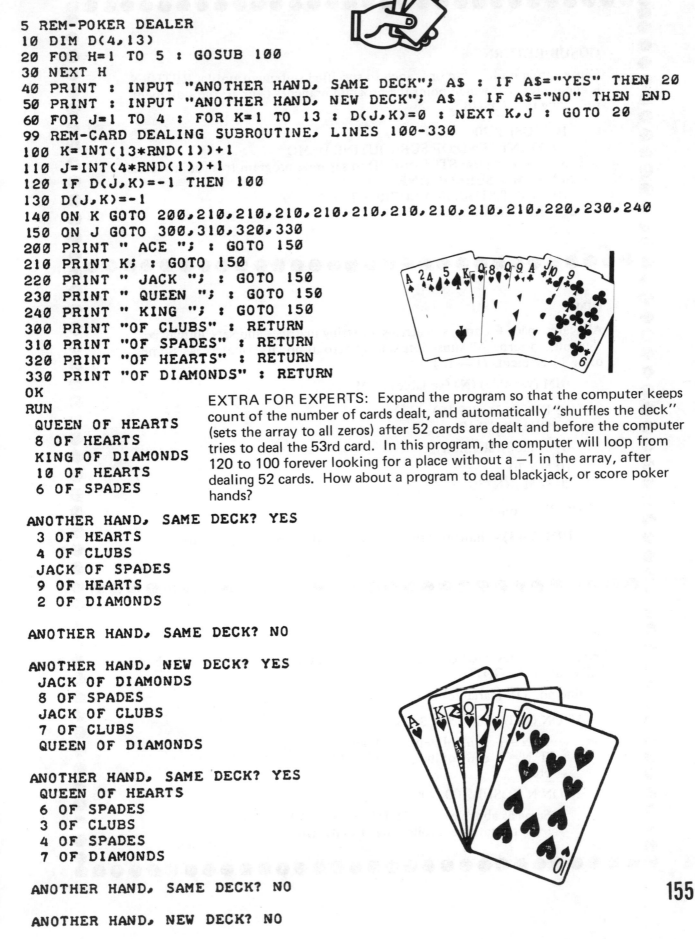

```
LIST

5 REM-POKER DEALER
10 DIM D(4,13)
20 FOR H=1 TO 5 : GOSUB 100
30 NEXT H
40 PRINT : INPUT "ANOTHER HAND, SAME DECK"; A$ : IF A$="YES" THEN 20
50 PRINT : INPUT "ANOTHER HAND, NEW DECK"; A$ : IF A$="NO" THEN END
60 FOR J=1 TO 4 : FOR K=1 TO 13 : D(J,K)=0 : NEXT K,J : GOTO 20
99 REM-CARD DEALING SUBROUTINE, LINES 100-330
100 K=INT(13*RND(1))+1
110 J=INT(4*RND(1))+1
120 IF D(J,K)=-1 THEN 100
130 D(J,K)=-1
140 ON K GOTO 200,210,210,210,210,210,210,210,210,210,220,230,240
150 ON J GOTO 300,310,320,330
200 PRINT " ACE "; : GOTO 150
210 PRINT K; : GOTO 150
220 PRINT " JACK "; : GOTO 150
230 PRINT " QUEEN "; : GOTO 150
240 PRINT " KING "; : GOTO 150
300 PRINT "OF CLUBS" : RETURN
310 PRINT "OF SPADES" : RETURN
320 PRINT "OF HEARTS" : RETURN
330 PRINT "OF DIAMONDS" : RETURN
OK
RUN
   QUEEN OF HEARTS
   8 OF HEARTS
   KING OF DIAMONDS
   10 OF HEARTS
   6 OF SPADES
```

EXTRA FOR EXPERTS: Expand the program so that the computer keeps count of the number of cards dealt, and automatically "shuffles the deck" (sets the array to all zeros) after 52 cards are dealt and before the computer tries to deal the 53rd card. In this program, the computer will loop from 120 to 100 forever looking for a place without a −1 in the array, after dealing 52 cards. How about a program to deal blackjack, or score poker hands?

```
ANOTHER HAND, SAME DECK? YES
   3 OF HEARTS
   4 OF CLUBS
   JACK OF SPADES
   9 OF HEARTS
   2 OF DIAMONDS

ANOTHER HAND, SAME DECK? NO

ANOTHER HAND, NEW DECK? YES
   JACK OF DIAMONDS
   8 OF SPADES
   JACK OF CLUBS
   7 OF CLUBS
   QUEEN OF DIAMONDS

ANOTHER HAND, SAME DECK? YES
   QUEEN OF HEARTS
   6 OF SPADES
   3 OF CLUBS
   4 OF SPADES
   7 OF DIAMONDS

ANOTHER HAND, SAME DECK? NO

ANOTHER HAND, NEW DECK? NO

OK
```

155

GOSUB/RETURN

Causes program to jump or branch to specified statement until a RETURN is encountered at which point the program branches back to the statement following the GOSUB.

```
 10  GOSUB 200
 20  PRINT "END OF SUBROUTINE DEMO"
 30  END     (Use STOP or END to separate program from subroutines)
200  REM – SUBROUTINE
210  PRINT "THIS IS A SUBROUTINE"
220  RETURN
```

DIM

Allocates space for arrays, matrices, or string matrices and sets all matrix elements to zero. All subscripts start at zero if no DIM, matrix is assumed to be 11 elements (1 − 10).

DIM (variable) (N) (variable) (N,M) ...

```
10 DIM A(3), B(5,10)
20 DIM N$(10,10)
```

Dynamic DIMension

```
10 N = 30
20 DIM X(N*30)
```

BASIC PLUS only

DIM A$(3) − indicates the number of strings, not length of one.

ON – GOTO

Jumps or branches (GOSUB) to the statement number indicated by the Nth number after the GOTO.

line no. ON (variable) GOTO line no., line no., line no.,

```
10 ON GOTO 100, 200, 300
```

If N = 1 control jumps to Line 100
If N = 2 control jumps to Line 200
etc.

```
20 ON N GOSUB 100, 200, 300
```

Same as above except RETURN from GOSUB branches back to statement following ON GOSUB.

CHAPTER 10 PROBLEMS

1. When do you use a DIM statement with two dimensional arrays?

2. You work in the personnel department of a large recreational facility like Disneyland. Your boss is under a lot of pressure from all over to demonstrate that you are an equal opportunity employer so he asks you to program the computer to prepare a report showing the sex and age breakdown of all employees. He provides the data as follows (you should put it in DATA statements in pairs).

Male = 1   Female = 2

Age
Under 21 = 1
21 — 29 = 2
30 — 39 = 3
40 — 49 = 4
50 — 59 = 5
over 60 = 6

```
-----------------------------------------------------------------

REPORT
AGE          MALE     FEMALE     TOTAL
UNDER 21
21 — 29
30 — 39
40 — 49
50 — 59
OVER 60
```

3. Sales Report 2: Remember the sales report for Nationwide Peddlers in Chapter 9? It lacked one element from being complete. Each of the six sales territories had three salesmen, each of whom report their sales to company headquarters. Reports are sent by phone indicating sales territory by number, salesman by number, and dollar sales. Write a program to accumulate these sales and print a nice report as shown.

Territory	Salesman 1	Salesman 2	Salesman 3	Totals
1				
2				
3				
4				
5				
6				

4. Shopping Guide: Pick 10 products by name, and size. Pick four stores. Go shop the stores and write down the prices of each item. Then write a computer program to make a report showing each store, it's prices, the total cost if you bought them all from one store. Experts will include an * next to the price that is the cheapest for each item. Place the information in DATA statements by store.

FUNCTIONS

RND(X) — generates a random number between 0 and 1

For RND in Altair BASIC, see pages 74–75.

Following functions apply to both ALTAIR BASIC and BASIC PLUS.

LEN(B$) — gives an integer equal to the number of characters in the string variable.

DEF FNA(A) — define your own function.

ABS(X) — gives absolute value of expression X.

INT(X) — gives largest integer less than or equal to argument X.

TAB(X) — spaces to the specified print column on the terminal.

USR(X) — calls machine language subroutine X.

FRE(0) — gives the number of bytes unused in memory.

SPC(X) — prints X number of blank spaces.

SGN(X) — gives 1 if X is greater than 0, zero if X is zero, and −1 if X is less than zero.

SIN(X) — gives sine of expression X if X is in radians.

SQR(X) — gives square root of X.

TAB(X) — spaces to the specified print column on terminal.

ATN(X) — gives arctangent of X in radians.

COS(X) — gives cosine of X in radians.

LOG(X) — gives natural (base e) log of X.

POS(X) — gives current position of terminal printhead.

DEF FN

Allows user to define functions.

        line no. DEF FN (variable name)(dummy variable) = function

BASIC PLUS only

FIX(X) — returns the truncated value of X.

LOG10(X) — gives common log of X.

PI — constant value of pi, 3.1415927

RND — generates a random number between 0 and 1. Same sequence each RUN. Use RANDOMIZE statement (10 RANDOMIZE) to change sequence.

STRING FUNCTIONS

BASIC PLUS only

INSTR(N1%, A$, B$) searches string A$ for substring B$ beginning at character N1 in string A$. Gives zero if substring not found. Gives character position if substring is found.

SPACE$(N%) — inserts N spaces within a string.

For Altair BASIC string functions, see pages 98–99.

Well, you have arrived at the end of the book, but you haven't arrived at the end of BASIC. Your computer system may use a version of BASIC with more capabilities than we have covered. And, we haven't even covered all of Altair 8K BASIC. However, if you understand and can use the BASIC instructions and functions we have introduced, you are well on your way. If you can do the end of chapter problems then you are really on your way to being able to write programs to meet your own needs.

Have fun and keep on hackin'.

The author would appreciate your comments, suggestions, and criticisms. Did you find mistakes? What confused you? Are there better ways to explain things? Better examples to use? We will continue to revise and improve this book before each printing, so your comments really will be read, and the author really will answer letters.

Thanks.

Jerald R. Brown   April, 1977
Dymax
P.O. Box 310
Menlo Park, CA 94025

THE END

The author holds a B.S. in psychology, and an M.Ed. in Research in Instruction from Harvard. He is Vice President of Dymax, and a co-founder of People's Computer Company and its spinoff, the Community Computer Center in Menlo Park, CA. He is co-author of BASIC by Albrecht, Finkel and Brown (Wiley, 1973) and other publications. He is also a filmmaker, and has done extensive educational television production.

159

INDEX

CHAPTER 1 SOLUTIONS

1.
```
10 PRINT "LISA STEWART"
20 PRINT"1826 GOLDEN AVE"
30 PRINT"REDWOOD CITY, CA"

RUN
LISA STEWART
1826 GOLDEN AVE
REDWOOD CITY, CA
```

2.
```
10 PRINT"LISA STEWART","1826 GOLDEN AVE","REDWOOD CITY,CA"
OK
RUN
LISA STEWART  1826 GOLDEN AVE           REDWOOD CITY,CA
```

3.
```
NEW
RETURN
OK
```

4.
```
LIST
RETURN
```

5. SHIFT   ←   (back arrow)

   or underline.

6.
```
OK
PRINT 172.16-13.50-19.00-3.25-10.00-114.14+87.51
 99.78
```

7.
```
10 LET T=(40+50+46+48+49+45+52+41+44+46)/10
20 PRINT "AVERAGE HEIGHT IS",T

RUN
AVERAGE HEIGHT IS            46.1
```

CHAPTER 2 SOLUTIONS

1.
```
LET
INPUT
READ
```

2. Quotation marks

3. Use direct mode

4.

A	B	C	D
12	0	0	0
12	14	0	0
12	14	16	0
12	14	16	0
12	14	16	5
12	14	16	5

5.
```
10 READ A$,B$,A
20 PRINT A$,B$,A
30 DATA "SHERRY DELIGHT","800-555-1212",23

RUN
SHERRY DELIGHT              800-555-1212   23
```

6.
```
10 INPUT"ENTER YOUR NAME";A$
20 INPUT "ENTER YOUR ASTROLOGICAL SIGN";S$
30 INPUT "ENTER YOUR BIRTHDATE";D$
40 PRINT A$,"YOU ARE UNDER THE SIGN OF ";S$
50 PRINT"SINCE YOUR BIRTHDAY IS ";D$

RUN
ENTER YOUR NAME? JERRY
ENTER YOUR ASTROLOGICAL SIGN? LEO
ENTER YOUR BIRTHDATE? 8/13/1950
JERRY           YOU ARE UNDER THE SIGN OF LEO
SINCE YOUR BIRTHDAY IS 8/13/1950
```

```
7.   10 LET X=(((4.80/.48)*100)*7.5)/150
     20 PRINT X,"MONTHS"
     OK
     RUN
      50              MONTHS


8.   20 INPUT"ENTER NO. OF SHOWERS PER DAY";S
     30 INPUT "ENTER NO. OF MINS. PER SHOWER";M
     40 INPUT"ENTER NO. OF TUB BATHS PER DAY";B
     50 INPUT"ENTER NO. OF HAND DISHWASHING JOBS/DAY";D
     60 INPUT"ENTER NO. OF AUTO. DISHWASHING JOBS/DAY";A
     70 INPUT"NO. OF TOILET FLUSHES/DAY";F
     80 INPUT"NO. OF WASHER LOADS/WEEK";W
     90 INPUT"NO. OF OUTDOOR HOSE MINUTES/DAY";H
     100 INPUT"ENTER NO. OF VARIOUS GALLONS USED/DAY";V
     110 LET T=0
     120 READ X
     130 LET T=T+(S*(M*X))*30
     140 READ X
     150 LET T=T+(B*X)*30
     160 READ X
     170 LET T=T+(D*X)*30
     180 READ X
     190 LET T=T+(A*X)*30
     200 READ X
     210 LET T=T+(F*X)*30
     220 READ X
     230 LET T=T+(W*X)*4.2
     240 READ X
     250 LET T=T+(H*X)*30
     260 LET T=T+(V*30)
     270 PRINT"YOU USE APPROX. "; T;"GALLONS / MONTH OR ";T/7.5; "CUBIC FEET
     280 PRINT"THAT IS AN AVERAGE OF ";T/30;"GALLONS PER DAY"
     300 DATA 6,20,15,16,6,35,10

     RUN
     ENTER NO. OF SHOWERS PER DAY? 1
     ENTER NO. OF MINS. PER SHOWER? 5
     ENTER NO. OF TUB BATHS PER DAY? 1
     ENTER NO. OF HAND DISHWASHING JOBS/DAY? 1
     ENTER NO. OF AUTO. DISHWASHING JOBS/DAY? 1
     NO. OF TOILET FLUSHES/DAY? 5
     NO. OF WASHER LOADS/WEEK? 3
     NO. OF OUTDOOR HOSE MINUTES/DAY? 0
     ENTER NO. OF VARIOUS GALLONS USED/DAY? 50
     YOU USE APPROX.  5271 GALLONS / MONTH OR   702.8 CUBIC FEET
     THAT IS AN AVERAGE OF  175.7 GALLONS PER DAY
```

CHAPTER 3 SOLUTIONS

1. 896700
    1,000,000,000,000,000
    1001
    61,576,200,000
    .00000387124

2. 1.78643E6
    3.1457E6
    1.2479E—4
    4.2456E—1

3. Press RETURN

4. CONTROL/C

```
5.   10 PRINT "NUMBER","SQUARED"
     20 LET T=1
     30 PRINT T,T↑2
     40 LET T=T+1
     50 GOTO 30


     NUMBER        SQUARED
       1              1
       2              4
       3              9
       4             16
       5             25
       6             36
       7             49
       8             64
       9             81
      10            100


6.   20 PRINT"F","C"
     30 LET F=30
     40 PRINT F,(5/9)*(F-32)
     50 LET F=F+1
     60 GOTO 40

     RUN
     F                C
       30           -1.11111
       31           -.555556
       32            0
       33            .555556
       34            1.11111
       35            1.66667
       36            2.22222
       37            2.77778
       38            3.33333
       39            3.88889
       40            4.44445
       41            5
       42            5.55556
```

CHAPTER 4 SOLUTIONS

No solutions provided.

CHAPTER 5 SOLUTIONS

1. Continues to the nearest statement in the program.

2. Not equal

3. Less than or equal to

4. No print statement and it branches to the same place (Line 30)
    if the condition is true or false.

5.
```
    10 INPUT "ENTER WATER USED IN GALLONS";G
    20 LET T=(G/7.5)/100:LET T=(T*.50)+2.85:PRINT"BILL IS "T:GOTO 10

    RUN
    ENTER WATER USED IN GALLONS? 6000
    BILL IS  6.85
    ENTER WATER USED IN GALLONS? 10000
    BILL IS  9.51667
    ENTER WATER USED IN GALLONS? 20000
    BILL IS  16.1833
    ENTER WATER USED IN GALLONS?
```

```
6.  10 INPUT "ENTER WATER USED IN GALLONS";G
    20 IF G<=8000 THEN PRINT "BILL IS "((G/7.5)/100)*.50+2.85:GOTO 10
    30 LET T=(((G-8000)/7.5)/100)*1.00
    40 LET T=T+((8000/7.5)/100)*.50+2.85:PRINT"BILL IS"T:GOTO 10

    RUN
    ENTER WATER USED IN GALLONS? 6000
    BILL IS  6.85
    ENTER  WATER USED IN GALLONS? 10000
    BILL IS 10.85
    ENTER WATER USED IN GALLONS? 20000
    BILL IS 24.1833
    ENTER WATER USED


7.  10 INPUT "HOW MANY MINUTES";M
    20 LET C=2.00:IF M<=45 THEN LET C=C+(M*.05):GOTO 40
    30 LET C=C+(45*.05)+(M-45)*.03
    40 PRINT"BILL IS "C: GOTO 10

    RUN
    HOW MANY MINUTES? 40
    BILL IS  4
    HOW MANY MINUTES? 45
    BILL IS  4.25
    HOW MANY MINUTES? 60
    BILL IS  4.7
    HOW MANY MINUTES? 100
    BILL IS  5.9
    HOW MANY MINUTES? ●DAD N$,Z$
    20 IF Z$="94061"THEN PRINTN$:GOTO 10
    30 GOTO 10
    40 DATA MARCUS,94025,LINDA, 94061, JERRY, 94061,LARRY,06542
    OK
    RUN
    LINDA
    JERRY
```

CHAPTER 6 SOLUTIONS

1. Negative value for X

2. 3, −4, 4, −5, 0, −1

3. 10 FOR X = 1 TO 30: ? INT(6*RND(1)) + 1 : NEXT

4. No solution

5.
```
    10 REM CRAPS
    20 LET A=INT(6*RND(1)+1):LET B=INT(6*RND(1)+1)
    25 PRINT"POINT IS "A+B
    30 IF A+B=7 THEN PRINT"WINNER":GOTO 20
    40 IF A+B=11 THEN PRINT"WINNER":GOTO 20
    50 LET C=INT(6*RND(1)+1):LET D=INT(6*RND(1)+1)
    55 PRINT C+D,
    60 IF A+B=C+DTHEN PRINT"WINNER":GOTO 20
    70 IF C+D=7 THEN PRINT"YOU CRAPPED OUT":GOTO 20
    80 GOTO 50

    RUN
    POINT IS  6
     4              5              10            4              8
     8              9              9             6              WINNER
    POINT IS  11
    WINNER
    POINT IS  6
     7              YOU CRAPPED OUT
    POINT IS  5
```

```
6.  10 REM STARS
    20 LET N=INT(100*RND(1)+1)
    30 INPUT"ENTER YOUR GUESS";G:IF G=N THEN PRINT"WINNER":GOTO 20
    40 LET D=ABS(G-N)
    50 IF D>=64 THEN 170
    60 IF D>=32 THEN 160
    70 IF D>=16 THEN 150
    80 IF D>=8 THEN 140
    90 IF D>=4 THEN 130
    100 IF D>=2 THEN 120
    110 PRINT"*";
    120 PRINT"*";
    130 PRINT"*";
    140 PRINT"*";
    150 PRINT"*";
    160 PRINT"*";
    170 PRINT"*":GOTO 30

    RUN
    ENTER YOUR GUESS? 50
    **
    ENTER YOUR GUESS? 25
    ****
    ENTER YOUR GUESS? 15
    *****
    ENTER YOUR GUESS? 10
    ******
    ENTER YOUR GUESS? 8
    ******
    ENTER YOUR GUESS? 12
    *******
    ENTER YOUR GUESS? 13
    ******
    ENTER YOUR GUESS? 11
    WINNER
    ENTER YOUR GUESS
```

CHAPTER 7 SOLUTIONS

1. It prints 17 and stops

2. A heading will keep printing each time through the loop. RND(0) gives
    the same number each time.

3. No solution.

4. 10 FOR X = 1 TO 72 : PRINT "*" ; NEXT

5.
```
    5 REM INTEREST TABLE
    8 PRINT"YEARS","5%","5.5%","6%","6.5%"
    10 FOR Y=5 TO 25 STEP 5
    15 PRINT Y,
    20 FOR I=5 TO 6.5 STEP .5
    30 PRINT 10000*(1+(I/100))↑Y,:NEXT I:PRINT
    40 NEXT Y
```

YEARS	5%	5.5%	6%	6.5%
5	12762.8	13069.6	13382.3	13700.9
10	16289	17081.4	17908.5	18771.4
15	20789.3	22324.7	23965.6	25718.4
20	26533	29177.5	32071.3	35236.5
25	33863.6	38133.7	42918.7	48277.1

6.
```
10 REM PAYROLL
15 PRINT"NAME","GROSS PAY"
20 READ N$,H,R
30 IF H<=40 THEN PRINTN$,H*R:GOTO 20
40 LET G=(40*R)+(H-40)*(R*1.5):PRINTN$,G: GOTO 20
900 DATA T. BOD, 40,4.00, T. RAY, 50, 4.00

RUN
NAME            GROSS PAY
T. BOD            160
T. RAY            220

?OD ERROR IN 20
OK
```

CHAPTER 8 SOLUTIONS

1. `10 DEF FNR(X)=INT(X*100+.5)/100`

2. BASIC IS BEST

3.
```
20 A$ = "INSTANT BASIC"
30 FOR X = LEN(A$) TO 1 STEP —1
40 PRINT MID(A$, X,X),
50 NEXT X
```

4.
```
10 READ N$
20 FOR X=1 TO LEN(N$)
30 IF MID$(N$,X,1)<>","THEN 60
40 PRINT MID$(N$,X+1),LEFT$(N$,X-1)
60 NEXT X
80 DATA"ZENITH,HAROLD"
```

5. No solution

6.
```
5 REM RANDOM NAME GENERATOR(CVCCVC)
10 V$="AEIOU":N$="BCDFGHJKLMNPQRSTVWXYZ"
15 FOR N=1 TO 20
20 V1=INT(5*RND(1))+1:V2=INT(5*RND(1))+1
30 C2=INT(21*RND(1))+1:C3=INT(21*RND(1))+1:C4=INT(21*RND(1))+1
40 PRINT"J";MID$(V$,V1,1);MID$(N$,C2,1);MID$(N$,C3,1);
45 PRINT MID$(V$,V2,1);MID$(N$,C4,1),
50 NEXT N
```

```
RUN
JIPFID       JUDBUV       JIDRID       JUHWEK       JEPTIZ
JOJWEB       JAXJOK       JEPSIG       JEZSUK       JIGNAV
JUSPOH       JEPXAT       JIYBOT       JUHLIF       JEMJEK
```

CHAPTER 9 SOLUTIONS

1. Line 70
   Print salesman name and total sales
   Tallies up grand total sales
   Line 100 or 110

2. L. FRENCH
   B. MIDLER
   14 00
   500

3. 16
   9
   9
   5

4. Only when your array exceeds 11 variables.

```
5.  20 READ P1,V1,T1:IF P1=-1 THEN 50
    30 P(P1)=P(P1)+1:V(V1)=V(V1)+1:T(T1)=T(T1)+1:GOTO 20
    50 PRINT"PRESIDENT","VEEP","TREASURER"
    60 FOR X=1 TO 3
    70 PRINTX;P(X),X;V(X),X;T(X)
    80 NEXT X
    90 DATA 1,1,1,2,2,2,3,3,3,1,2,3,3,2,1,2,1,3,2,2,3,1,2,1,-1,-1,-1
```

```
RUN
PRESIDENT        VEEP              TREASURER
    1   3           1   2              1   3
    2   3           2   5              2   1
    3   2           3   1              3   4
```

```
6.  10 REM GRADE COUNTER
    15 PRINT"GRADE","NUMBER"
    20 READ G:IF G=-1 THEN 30
    25 C(G)=C(G)+1:GOTO 20
    30 FOR X=1 TO 5:PRINTX,C(X):NEXT X
    40 PRINT "A'S AND B'S TOTAL",C(4)+C(3)
    50 DATA 4,4,3,3,2,2,1,1,3,3,4,4,4,3,2,3,4,-1
```

```
RUN
GRADE            NUMBER
    1               2
    2               3
    3               6
    4               6
    5               0
A'S AND B'S TOTAL              12
```

```
7.  5 REM SLOT MACHINE
    10 FOR X=1 TO 5:READ N$(X):NEXT X
    20 FOR X=1 TO 3:A(X)=INT(5*RND(1))+1:NEXT X
    30 FOR X=1 TO 3:PRINT N$(A(X)),:NEXT X
    55 REM DOUBLE /TRIPLE TEST
    60 IF A(1)<>A(2) THEN 80
    65 IF A(2)<>A(3)THEN 70
    66 IF A(1)=5 THEN PRINT"BIG WINNER. TAKE $1.00":GOTO 20
    67 PRINT"3 IN A ROW. $.25":GOTO 20
    70 PRINT"YOU WIN $.10":GOTO 20
    75 REM CHERRY TEST
    80 IF A(1)=1 THEN PRINT"YOU WIN $.05":GOTO 20
    90 PRINT"NOTHING WON. NEXT NICKEL":GOTO 20
    100 DATA CHERRY,PEACH,PLUM,APPLE,BAR
```

```
RUN
PLUM          PEACH         APPLE         NOTHING WON. NEXT NICKEL
CHERRY        BAR           APPLE         YOU WIN $.05
APPLE         PLUM          PEACH         NOTHING WON. NEXT NICKEL
BAR           PLUM          PLUM          NOTHING WON. NEXT NICKEL
CHERRY        BAR           PLUM          YOU WIN $.05
PEACH         BAR           APPLE         NOTHING WON. NEXT NICKEL
APPLE         APPLE         BAR           YOU WIN $.10
BAR           APPLE         BAR
```

1. Always

2.
```
10 REM EQUAL OPPORTUNITY
15 DIM C(6,2)
20 READ S,A:IF S=-1 THEN 40
30 C(A,S)=C(A,S)+1:C(0,S)=C(0,S)+1:C(A,0)=C(A,0)+1:GOTO 20
40 PRINT"AGE","MALE","FEMALE","TOTAL"
50 FOR A=1 TO 6:READ D$:PRINTD$,
60 FOR S=1 TO 2:PRINT C(A,S),:NEXT S
70 PRINTC(A,0):NEXT A
80 PRINT"TOTALS",C(0,1),C(0,2)
90 DATA 1,3,2,2,1,1,2,4,2,5,2,6,1,6,1,5,1,4,1,3,1,2,1,2,-1,-1
100 DATA UNDER 21,21-29,30-39,40-49,50-59,OVER 59
```

RUN

AGE	MALE	FEMALE	TOTAL
UNDER 21	1	0	1
21-29	2	1	3
30-39	2	0	2
40-49	1	1	2
50-59	1	1	2
OVER 59	1	1	2
TOTALS	8	4	

3.
```
10 REM SALES REPORT 2
20 DIM G(6,3)
30 READ T,S,D:IF T=-1 THEN 50
40 G(T,S)=G(T,S)+D:G(T,0)=G(T,0)+D:GOTO 30
50 PRINT"TERRITORY","SALNO1","SALNO2","SALNO3","TOTAL"
60 FOR T=1 TO 6:PRINTT,
70 FOR S=1 TO 3:PRINTG(T,S),:NEXT S:PRINTG(T,0):NEXT T
90 DATA 1,1,500,2,1,1000,3,1,200,2,1,150,2,1,400,2,3,500
100 DATA 3,1,1000,3,2,2000,3,3,1500,4,1,1500,4,2,1500,4,3,2000
110 DATA 5,1,100,5,2,100,5,3,100
120 DATA 6,1,650,6,2,760,6,3,800
130 DATA -1,-1,-1
```

RUN

TERRITORY	SALNO1	SALNO2	SALNO3	TOTAL
1	500	0	0	500
2	1550	0	500	2050
3	1200	2000	1500	4700
4	1500	1500	2000	5000
5	100	100	100	300
6	650	760	800	2210

4.
```
10 REM SHOPPING GUIDE
15 DIM P(10,4),T(4)
18 REM READ IN DATA
20 FOR S=1 TO 4
30 FOR I=1 TO 10: READ P(I,S):NEXT I:NEXT S
40 REM PRINT IT OUT
50 PRINT"ITEM #","STORE1",2,3,4
60 FOR I=1 TO 10:PRINTI,
70 FOR S=1 TO 4:PRINTP(I,S),:T(S)=T(S)+P(I,S):NEXT S
80 NEXT I
90 PRINT"TOTALS",:FOR X=1 TO 4:PRINTT(X),:NEXT X
100 DATA 1,2,3,4,5,6,7,8,9,10
110 DATA 10,9,8,7,6,5,4,4,2,1
120 DATA 1,1,2,2,3,3,4,4,5,5
130 DATA4,4,5,5,6,6,7,7,8,8
```

ITEM #	STORE1	2	3	4
1	1	10	1	4
2	2	9	1	4
3	3	8	2	5
4	4	7	2	5
5	5	6	3	6
6	6	5	3	6
7	7	4	4	7
8	8	4	4	7
9	9	2	5	8
10	10	1	5	8
TOTALS	55	56	30	60

ERRATA

All references to Altair BASIC can be read as references to MICROSOFT™ BASIC.

Page 3. Sixth line should read, "Sometimes it is just labelled "CR," or ENTER, or GO . . .

Page 13. The back arrow and letter O key in the line above the keyboard is printed upside down. It should look the same as the key to the left of the keyboard.

Page 36. Problem 4, line 6 should read: 50 LET D = (B + C)/6

Page 47. The first paragraph should continue, "(BASIC PLUS may only accept a variable with 2 characters where the first is a letter and the second a digit.)"

Page 49. The first paragraph should continue, "For BASIC PLUS, try the ampersand, that is, & ("and" sign)."

The remarks for line 20 of the program list should continue, "(Not true for BASIC PLUS or some other versions of BASIC.)"

Page 53. Lines 6, 7, and 8 should read as follows:

```
10 IF X < 10 THEN 50
10 IF X < 10 THEN PRINT "NUMBER IS LESS THAN 10"
10 IF X > 10 THEN PRINT "ERROR" : X = 0 : GO TO 50
```

Page 73. First paragraph should continue, "Note: in many versions of BASIC, you get a random <u>digit</u> between 1 and whatever positive whole number you put in the parentheses, eg., RND (10) produces random digits between 1 and 10 inclusive."

Page 79. Line 10 should read, "Line 430 prints TOO SMALL if the Guess G is smaller than X."

Line 14 should read, "Line 440 prints TOO BIG, because of the guess is not equal to or smaller than the computer's number X, then it must be bigger. The computer doesn't need an IF statement to decide that!"

Page 80. Problem 6 should read "STARS".

Line 8 of Problem 6 should read, "Logic: If the guess is 64 or more away, . . .

The last line should continue, "(See page 116.)"

Page 116. Second sentence should read, "SGN( ) stands for SiGN, and gives you a plus 1 (+1), a zero, or a minus 1 (-1), depending on whether the value considered in the parentheses is positive, zero, or negative."

Page 118. Line 13 should read, "regular variables and string variables (see page 46 . . ."

Page 130. Line 5 under BABY NEEDS A NEW PAIR . . . should read as follows:
5 FOR J=1 TO 6 : T(J)=0 : NEXT J

Line 60 should read:
6Ø FOR K=1 TO 6 : ? K; "'S:"; T(K) : NEXT K : ? : GOTO 5

Page 136. Variable 9 should be S4, not S$.

Page 137. Line 100 should be:
100 S=S+S4 : IF S4<=3500 THEN PRINT 700 : S1=S1+700 : GOTO 40

The salary for P.PADRE should be 700 and the total salaries should be 3700.42.

Page 147. Line 28 should read "beginning of each line in the table. See page 92."

Page 152. Last paragraph should continue "This is not so in other versions of BASIC, so experiment!"

Page 153. Line 5 of second paragraph should read "is negative, or is zero, OR is bigger than the number of line . . ."

Page 156. Line 4 of DIM should read "to be 11 elements (0 - 10)."

Line 5 of ON-GOTO should read as follows:
10 ON N GOTO 100, 200, 300

Page 158. Line 5 from bottom should read as follows:
INSTR(N1$,A$,B$) . . .

Line 2 from bottom should read as follows:
SPACE(N$) . . .

Solutions at back of book:

Chapter 1. Number 7 should read:
10 PRINT "AVERAGE HEIGHT IS", (40+50+46+48+49+45+52+41+46)/10

RUN
AVERAGE HEIGHT IS   46.1

Chapter 2. Number 2 should read "By quotation marks."

Chapter 3. Number 3 should read "Press RETURN or its equivalent on your keyboard."

Chapter 4. Should read "No solutions provided, do your own."

Chapter 5. Number 7, Run should end after fifth "HOW MANY MINUTES".

Number 8 should begin with 10 READ N$,Z$

Chapter 6. Number 4 should read "No solution provided, do your own."

Chapter 7. Number 3 should read "No solution provided, do your own."

Chapter 8. Number 5 should read "No solution provided, do your own."